The Gospel According to a Mountain Momma

by

Paul Dodd

McClain Printing Company
Parsons, West Virginia 26287
www.mcclainprinting.com
2002

International Standard Book Number 0-87012-683-0
Library of Congress Control Number 2002093305
Printed in the United States of America
Copyright © 2002 by Paul Dodd
Baldwinsville, NY
All Rights Reserved
2002

Reprinted 2005

Printed by
McClain Printing Company
Parsons, WV 26287
www.mcclainprinting.com
2005

CONTENTS

FOREWORD

This book is a tribute, not just to my Momma, but to all the unselfish, loving mothers who have worked hard and sacrificed during tough times in order to provide their children a home, the necessities of life, and an opportunity for a bright future.

I used my Momma as the focus for the book because, naturally, she is the example that I know best. She was a true daughter of the Appalachian Mountains. She loved her part of the world which was primarily Raleigh and Summers Counties in West Virginia. Her faith and her values were deeply rooted in the local culture which included family, church, and community. She was so many things. She was a loving mother, master gardener, fantastic cook, dedicated Bible scholar, tireless church worker, and a sympathetic, caring nurse. She could sing like an angel and she could do the work of a farm hand.

Her desire was to be Christ-like, and she achieved her goal in many, many ways. She calmed the storms around her with a soft word, she aided in the healing of sick people by her presence and prayers, she fed every hungry person who ever asked her for food, and she walked miles and miles to visit the lonely.

But as great as she was, she was not alone in her greatness. I think of her contemporaries in our little hollow community and I recognize the same greatness in all of them; different personalities and somewhat different circumstances, but the same loving, sacrificial commitment to their homes and families.

I remember the mothers of our community, women with great names like Nellie, Nora, Ida, Bessie, Ethel, Piney, Iris, Nettie, Lucille, Ruth, Ruby, Frances, Georgia, Gladys, Gracie, Reba, Della, Evelyn, Mattie, Orene, Glenna, Violet, Lucy, and Pearl, any one of which I would have trusted with my life.

But all the great mothers did not live just in our community; instead, they are just one small locality's contribution to the greatest civilizing force in our world; humble, hardworking, praying mothers.

While working in New York State, I heard Governor Mario Cuomo speak many times and I never heard him fail to pay tribute to his mother. He always cited her young life on a farm in Italy and how she constantly reminded him of the importance of being close to the land and staying close to God. Nearly all of us, like him, are indebted to our "foremothers" who left their native countries and braved the hardships of a new culture, new language, and great uncertainty, and with their faith and hard work laid the foundations for our families. Some of us may have had "foremothers" who lived through the horror of slavery, praying and hoping for freedom and opportunity for their children and descendents.

The pioneer mother who crossed the country in a covered wagon, the mother who lived in a tent in the blistering Nevada sun while her husband helped build the Boulder Dam, the mother who waited with her children at the mouth of a mine after an explosion to see if their Dad survived, the inner city mother who worked two jobs to feed her children, and the Appalachia mother who sacrificed all of her life so her children could have a better opportunity; these are examples of the mothers that I want to honor with this book.

THE GOSPEL ACCORDING TO A MOUNTAIN MOMMA

1   MOMMA'S LOVE STORY . . . AS TOLD BY DAD

"Arthur worked all day in town. It is cold tonight and snowing some. We have a good fire and enjoyed the evening together - talking and studying our Sunday School lesson."
Momma's diary: Saturday, February 1, 1958

Momma died on the day after Thanksgiving, in 1976.

Rose and I had gone with Dad to spend Thanksgiving Day with her at the nursing home at Denmar, deep in the mountains of Pocahontas County, West Virginia.

It was one of those bright, sunny fall days and as we drove from Summers County we were treated to the magnificent beauty that is West Virginia in the fall. The autumn leaves had changed from their earlier bright colors of yellow and gold to the more sedate, deeper colors of crimson and orange and stood out in sharp contrast to the rich green background provided by the hemlocks and pines. The pastures fields of the limestone region from Alderson to Lewisburg were bright green as the bluegrass had responded to the fall rains and cooler temperatures and cattle of all hues were grazing on the hillsides and plateaus along the way.

When we arrived and entered the nursing home, we experienced an abrupt shift from the beauty of the outdoors to the stark reality of Momma's world. The atmosphere in the nursing home, as in all similar facilities, with the sounds, smells, and sights of the severely impaired residents was, to me, overwhelmingly depressing.

When we got to Momma's room, we could not tell if she knew that we were there because she was not able to communicate with us. She had suffered from Parkinson's Disease for years and had lapsed into a coma in August.

It was heart breaking to look down at Momma just lying there. She was so tiny, she now weighed less than seventy pounds, and her body was as rigid as stone and drawn into a severe bowed shape. She stared blankly out into space and her mouth was open wide. Her only movement was her hands constantly feeling the buttons on the front of her dressing gown.

We spent Thanksgiving Day in her room, talking to her, touching her, feeding her as best we could, hoping and praying that in some way we were being of help or comfort to her.

This was an unusual day for Rose and me because we lived six hundred miles away and had not previously visited Momma in the nursing home. The last time we had seen her was at the home place in August when her condition had worsened and she became comatose. But this was not an unusual day for Dad. Nearly every day since he had resigned himself to the fact that she must have the care of a nursing facility and admitted her, he had driven the sixty miles or so from the old home place to Denmar to be with her.

Before we had left to visit Momma the next day, the day after Thanksgiving, Dad received a call that her condition had become critical and that we should come at once. We called my two sisters and we all immediately went to the nursing home only to find that Momma had passed away before we got there.

The rest of the day was spent in the haze of contacting the Lobban Funeral Home in Alderson, the sad drive back to the funeral home, selecting a casket, deciding what Momma would wear, arranging for the services and burial, and carrying out the other numerous details in preparing for one of the most dreaded events in a person's life; the funeral of one's own Mother.

By the time Dad, Rose, and I arrived back at the home place that night it was nearly 10 o'clock. We had not had anything to eat since breakfast so Rose and I went into the kitchen to prepare a snack. When we asked Dad to come into the kitchen and eat, he said he wasn't hungry. However, he did agree to come and sit at the table with us while we ate. Soon after he sat down, he began talking:

"I want to tell you kids something. I'm the luckiest man on the face of the earth." Then he paused for a long time as he stared off into space. After a while, he started again.

"I was married for 58 years to the only woman that I ever wanted and I have not figured out to this day what she ever saw in me.

"You know that Bertha was three years older than me, and I never thought I would have a chance with her. She was the prettiest girl in the whole country and she could have had anybody she wanted.

"The first time I started talking to her was when I was about 17 and it was at a wake for one of our neighbors in Jumping Branch. In that day and time, when somebody died, people would gather in from all around and stay up all night at the house where the person lay a corpse. People who could sing would get together and make up a choir. Me and Bertha were both singers and so we sang in the choir off and on all night. Then after the funeral the next day, I got up all the nerve I had and I asked her if I could walk her home.

"She lived at Pluto, all the way down on Pinch Creek, but when she said I could walk her home, I just took off with her and didn't tell nobody where I was going or when I'd be back.

"It was after dark when we got to her house and we were tired and hungry so her Mother fixed us a bite of supper and then Bertha took me to sit in the parlor and the rest of the family just left us alone. I sprawled out there on the davenport and she pulled a rocking chair up close to the davenport and sat next to me. The next thing I knew, I heard a rooster crowing and I knew that it was morning. I looked up and Bertha was sitting there asleep in the chair. I woke her up and told her that I had to be going and I hit 'em out up the mountain for home.

"It was way up in the middle of the day by the time I got home and my Mother was waiting for me. She wanted to know where I'd been, and she didn't believe a word of it when I told her that I had been to preacher George Meador's house in Pluto and that I fell asleep in his parlor. Not even my own Mother thought that Bertha would be interested in me and she accused me of lying and that I had stayed out all night with a girl there in Jumping Branch that had a bad reputation.

"As soon as the word got out that I had walked Bertha home, the other boys just hooted. They said, 'Why are you going after her, you'll never get her. She's Henry Brammer's girl! Henry can have her any time he wants her. All he's got to do is snap his fingers.'

"Now, Henry Brammer had the most to offer of any man around. He had plenty of money and I didn't have a dime. He had a different suit of clothes for every day in the week and I didn't have but one suit to my name. He was one of the few people that I knew that had a car and I didn't even have my own riding horse. He was twenty-five years old and I was only seventeen. So I knew what the other boys were saying was probably true, but all I knew was that I was going to keep on going to see her as long as she didn't tell me she didn't want to see me any more.

"Then Bertha invited me over to her church in Pluto one night for some kind of a program that she was in, and as soon as I got there I knew that I was in hot water. The first thing I saw was Henry Brammer's big automobile, parked there in front of the church with all the horses and buggies. The first thing I thought of doing was to turn around and head for home but I said to myself, 'No sir, I'm going to stay and see what happens,' so I slipped in as quiet as I could and sat down on the back row.

"Bertha was in charge of the program so she was up front during the whole service. Henry was sitting up there, as big as you please, in the third row right next to the center aisle. As soon as the program was over and Bertha started to walk to the back of the church, Henry stood up and took her arm and told her that he was there to see her home.

"When I saw this happening, my heart stopped beating, and I was gonna sneak out of there as fast as I could. But then I heard her say, loud enough for everybody to hear, 'You will have to excuse me Henry, I have other company here tonight.' Then she walked on back and took me by the arm and we left the church together. I'm telling you the truth, I felt like I was the biggest man on earth that night.

"You know, she really could have had Henry Brammer and I worried a lot about that over the years because I knew that she would have been a lot better off if she had picked him instead of me. He had a lot of money and you know that we never had nothing. He was a big politician and even became the High Sheriff of Raleigh County. One time, after we had been married probably thirty or forty years, when we were driving past his big brick house over toward Beckley, I told Bertha that she could be living in that house. When I said that, she scooted over as close to me as she could, patted me on the leg, and said 'I'm just fine, thank you.' "

I learned more that night than I had ever known about the love affair that was my parent's life together. I could now better understand how two people could live together for more than a half century and never have a serious fight. I could also better understand the respect that Dad had always showed to Momma and his unwavering devotion to her, through both the good years of making a life together, and through the bad years of her gradual death.

As a child, I was uncomfortable with the fact that Momma was older than Dad but now I was able to see that this had been a key factor in their love story. Dad had not believed that he deserved Momma and had always placed her on a pedestal. Love is funny, in a way, in that if someone great loves you and you do not feel that you deserve it, you may spend your entire life trying to be worthy of that love, and that is what Dad had done. So now I saw something that Dad could not see; his undying love and devotion to her had made him the best possible choice for a lifetime mate for her.

The next morning after my sisters arrived at the house, I encouraged Dad to relate the story to them. He made a weak attempt, but his heart was not in it. He had relived it vividly on the night she died, relating it one time, not really to Rose and me, but rather to himself and his memory of Momma.

Now he seemed more interested in getting on with his responsibilities in laying to rest his beloved.

"I am so thankful for my dear companion, who has been very sweet and kind through the years."
Momma's diary on her birthday: January 2, 1959

2   WHO WAS MOMMA AND WHERE DID SHE COME FROM?

"Arthur brought news that Athel was dead. Sure was sad news."
Momma's diary: Saturday February 22, 1958

"We went to Beckley today. Got a treatment and then visited Lura and Beulah. We ate dinner with Lura, Clyde, Hallie, Maude, and Claude. We felt sad as Athel was being buried at 2 o'clock."
Momma's diary: Monday February 24, 1958

My uncle Athel was Mom's oldest full brother and I never met him. When he became an adult, he had left home to work on the railroad just like his older half-brothers. He lived and died in Montana, and never returned, even for a visit. None of the family considered making the long trip to attend the funeral of the brother they had not seen for over forty years, but, as Momma noted in her diary, some of them were able to be together at the time of his services.

I was with Momma the day she heard that her half-brother, Elbert, had died in Oklahoma, and I remember that she sat down at the kitchen table, cried softly, and remarked that "he was such a sweet brother." The only contact that she had had with him for more than forty years was their exchange of Christmas cards with a short personal note and an occasional picture..

Was Momma tough? Resilient? Born of sturdy stock? Yes, but also very fragile in many ways. The treatment that she spoke of in her February 24 diary entry was her regular visit to a psychiatrist who was treating her for extreme anxiety and nervousness. I will discuss that more fully later.

Who was Momma? What made her the person she was and how, more than twenty five years since her passing, can I better define her and understand her?

"Jan. 2nd which is my 62nd birthday. Paul started back about 9 this morning. I hated for him to leave as I always miss him so much. Dad is working as usual. It is a beautiful day but cold. Leora and David came and ate dinner with us. **Brought me a Diary** *for my birthday which was nice and very thoughtful. "*

Momma's diary: January 2, 1958

I have used many sources to help me define Momma. Fortunately, her daughter, Leora, gave her a diary as a birthday gift in which she kept a daily record of her activities and thoughts for two years, from 1958 to 1960, from her sixty-second birthday until her sixty-fourth, to the day. These were years when I was not with her very much since I was in college, so her diary was a treasure trove of information. Another source was miscellaneous writings which she left in her Bibles.

However, my memory, which is good although selective, is my primary source. I remember her in so many ways, as do my two sisters, Leora and Rhodetta, who have shared their memories with me.

We also knew many of Momma's brothers and sisters who were products of the same environment and our memories of their personalities and opinions help shed some light on her early, formative years. Her parents had both died years before I was born so I only heard about them, but what I heard also added to the information from which I could draw some conclusions.

One very unexpected source of understanding has come, strangely enough, from my two granddaughters, Lisa and Sarah. Born decades after Momma's death, they have given me insights which I never had previously.

One day, when Lisa was not yet two years old, she set out to follow her big brother, Jeremy, through the woods behind our house to the maple tree that Jeremy liked to climb. Knowing that there were briers, dead limbs, and other barriers that would impede the progress of a toddler, I called to her to stop and ran to rescue her. By the time I got to her, she was making amazing progress, not due to her skill but, rather, due to her determination.

Instead of rescuing her, I just stood dumbstruck as the realization hit me, "there goes my Momma." Lisa had decided on what she believed to be the correct course of action and she was determined not to let any obstacle or hardship prevent her from carrying it out. The way she moved, the way she held her head, the way she kept on going even when the going got rough: I saw Momma in her!

Momma was the eleventh of George Washington Meador's eighteen children.

Her father, a circuit riding preacher, had lost his wife, Virginia Upton, to tuberculosis on January 11, 1885, three months after the birth of their sixth child, a little girl named Minty. Seven months later, Minty also died. Now a single parent with five rambunctious boys ranging in age from four to thirteen, Brother George Meador lost little time before starting to look for a new wife.

One bright sunny Sunday morning in a church yard in Ballard, West Virginia, in 1886, a small group of teenage girls were talking together as they awaited the arrival of the new preacher. They were excited when they saw a slender man riding on a black horse coming over the hill toward the church.

As he came closer and the girls could see the man in the black suit with his well trimmed moustache and wavy hair, they quickly agreed that this was the most handsome man they had ever seen. Momma said that my grandmother told her that "all of us girls set our caps for him right then and there," and she was the one he chose.

When George Meador and Rhoda Jane Crotty were married in 1887, he was thirty-two and she was exactly half his age, just sixteen.

They settled in the community of Pluto, in Raleigh County where George and Virginia had started building a house. They had completed only two rooms by the time of Virginia's death, so George, Rhoda Jane, and sons Charles, Nelson, Elbert, Azil, and Simon, began adding onto the house located in a narrow valley carved out of the hills by Pinch Creek. They, of necessity, earned their livelihood "by the sweat of their brow" on their rugged, hillside farm. Circuit riding preachers did not get paid much. The farm had to feed and support their already large, but soon to get larger, family.

Rhoda Jane's first child, Maude, was born in 1889, then Athel in 1891, Lura in 1892, Rheo in 1894, Bertha (Momma) in 1896, Annie (who died as an infant) in 1898, Una in 1899, Clyde in 1900, Guy in 1903, Claude in 1905, Beulah in 1908, and, finally, Russell in 1910. She had twelve children in twenty-one years.

Momma was her father's eleventh child and her mother's fifth child. When she was born, her half-brother Charles was twenty-two years old. Her half-brother, Elbert, whose death I saw her quietly mourn and call "such a sweet brother," was seventeen and probably had left home by the time she was two or three.

Being in a family with nine older living siblings and six younger living siblings, working to survive on a subsistence farm in the heart of the Appalachian mountains at the turn of the twentieth century - what was that life like?

It was hard. It was stark. It was tough. We do not have much of a basis for comparison in the modern United States. If we were to look for comparisons, we would have to go to some other part of the world where modernization and development have not taken place.

Those who experienced the hardships of this type of life were greatly affected by it. Some became misers and hoarders so they would never be poor again. Some left this harsh environment, never to return.

The effects on Momma seemed to be that she learned how to not be intimidated by hardship or deprivation. She could summon tremendous strength during a crisis, and she had great compassion for the poor and suffering. Somehow, Momma's early life produced in her the qualities of humility, generosity, and sacrificial concern for others. I am not sure how it happened, but I will discuss some of the situations and events which seem to me to be significant.

I am a person who values privacy. I can only imagine the lack of privacy at Momma's girlhood home with as many as nineteen people living in one small house. The upstairs in the house that her parents built was originally one large room until the girls started coming of age, and then a partition was erected down the middle creating one room for the boys and one for the girls.

Both George and Rhoda Jane came from large families so relatives were frequent visitors in the home. Visiting preachers were always made welcome and Momma talked fondly of the visits by the Bishops, who she described as very Godly, spiritual men. A house full of parents, brothers, sisters, relatives, preachers, and even an occasional Bishop; no opportunities for privacy there.

When I was small, Momma kept a large box of old clothes in the corner of her bedroom. She would cut up those clothes during the winter and make patchwork quilts and crocheted rugs. Once, when I had climbed up into the box and sank into the softness, she told me that when she was a little girl and they had company, she would try to be the first to get to her mother's similar old clothing box so she could sleep there, rather than on the floor or in the same bed with numerous other people.

Also related to privacy, I am now going to discuss a squeamish subject, so if you are of a delicate nature, you may want to skip the next few paragraphs.

I have lived long enough and been sufficiently blessed that I can occupy one bathroom in our home while Rose occupies another, and we have a spare beyond that if there is an emergency. My life has not always been this luxurious, though. During the first eight years of my childhood, we had the proverbial seven rooms and a path. We had a privy, an outhouse, or, if you prefer, a "parlor out back."

It was a beauty. Built of sturdy oak, it had two seats and a good ventilation system. It was built to specifications developed by the United States government which were distributed widely during the early years of Franklin Delano Roosevelt's presidency and was like millions of other outhouses which were built to the same specifications, and sometimes, even, with labor provided by the Works Projects Administration (WPA) crews. My ninth grade civics teacher, Robert E. Via, who was not a great admirer of FDR, said that one good thing that he did for the country was to help provide sanitary toilet facilities for millions of people.

Of course, the home in which Momma grew up did not have an indoor bathroom. I was chagrined to find out, though, that they did an outdoor one, either. My Momma grew up in a home that did not even have an outhouse!

After I gave it some thought I realized that even if they did have one, there would have been big problems with nineteen people lining up to get into it. Even if it was a two seater and they lined up in pairs. But still; no outhouse? Mr. Via was right; FDR did the country a great service.

Prior to 1932, and certainly before the turn of the twentieth century, in the part of the country where Momma was raised, outhouses were probably the exception rather than the rule. And they did not have one. I got this great bit of information from Uncle Claude, Momma's younger bachelor brother who often spent summers with us, working on the farm. Uncle Claude had a strange habit of taking corn cobs with him to the outhouse. Observing this curious behavior, I inquired about it. He then gave me some eye-opening information about life before outhouses, before toilet paper, and even before Sears-Roebuck catalogs.

When I confronted Momma with Uncle Claude's disturbing revelations, she told me that they had to use the wooded area behind their house as their "outhouse." She said that even when she was very small, she would seek out a private place for herself in the woods. This conversation came back to me very clearly one day when my granddaughter, Sarah, at age two needed my help in going to the bathroom. She wanted me to place her smaller seat on the commode and then she said sternly, "you go, Pa-Paw, I can do it myself." I could very clearly imagine the concerns of my modest mother as a little girl as I observed the modesty and independence of Sarah, almost exactly a century later.

"Has been a pretty day. I have been right busy doing first one thing and then another. Stretched two pairs of curtains, planted some corn and beans. Rested awhile in the afternoon. The cow was fresh.
(Author's note: a calf was born)
Momma's diary: May 13, 1958

Hard work seemed to come natural to Momma. She gave birth to, and mothered, five children. She did the washing on Monday, the ironing on Tuesday, cleaned the church on Thursday, and cooked all day Saturday. She, almost single-handedly, raised a half acre garden each year which included the planting, hoeing, weeding, harvesting, cooking, and canning. She grew lettuce, radishes, cabbage, corn, beans, peas, tomatoes, squash, cucumbers, peppers, beets, greens, melons, turnips, parsnips, onions, peanuts, and occasionally tried something different like celery or okra.

From the bounty of this garden, in addition to feeding us well all summer, she canned corn, beans, and peas; she made beet and cucumber pickles; she filled large crock jars with sauerkraut, pickled corn, and pickled beans; she strung green beans and hung them to dry to make "leather britches;" she parched corn by drying it on a window screen cantilevered over the cook stove, weighted down by her flat irons (she made dried apples in the same way); and she made preserves from the ground cherries that grew wild in the garden. Nothing went to waste.

"Claude gathered a lot of apples for himself and us. I put up several jars. I pick a bucket of beans most every day and work them up. Have the freezer just about filled up. I love to put up things for winter. God has blessed us with plenty.

Momma's diary: August 25, 1959

As if taking care of her garden was not enough hard work, she climbed mountains and trees and so she could pick, process, and preserve cherries, raspberries, blackberries, huckleberries, grapes, apples, peaches, and pears. She made great kettles of apple butter and homemade soap (at different times and in different kettles, of course); and was a full working partner with Dad for six weeks each fall as they made the sorghum molasses for the entire countryside.

She made clothes, quilts, curtains, and rugs, and still found the time to clean the church each week and visit the sick. And she did this, and much more, without electricity or running water for most of the first twenty-eight years of her marriage.

I never heard Momma complain about the work that she was required to do as a child, but her sister, my Aunt Maude, sure complained. Aunt Maude said that their Papa was a harsh, unfeeling man who worked his children from sunup to sundown like slaves, and that no consideration or special treatment was given to the girls; they were expected to do as much work as the boys. She said that it was no wonder that, as soon as they were old enough, all the boys left home, some to never return. The sad thing, according to her, was that the girls had no choice but to wait until they got married to leave home. The childhood experiences left Aunt Maude, and possibly some of the others, very bitter.

But Momma never complained about the hard work they were expected to do. She told me that her favorite activity, as a child, was fishing. She said that after working in the fields all morning, they would come to the house for dinner, their big noon meal. When her Papa had finished eating, he would go sit in his rocking chair and take a thirty minute nap before rounding up the kids and returning to the fields. She said that she would eat her meal as fast as she could and then grab her fishing pole and run to the creek near their house for a few minutes of pure delight.

She said that when she caught any fish, even if they were small, her mother would clean them that afternoon and they would be served at supper, their evening meal. She said that her Papa loved fish and had the unusual ability to eat the small fish, bones and all.

My granddaughter Lisa has helped me visualize this happening. Lisa keeps her fishing pole at our house and on those occasions when her parents are busy and she comes to our house for an hour or so after school, she often grabs her pole, jumps on her bicycle, and dashes madly for the pond in our neighborhood for her moments of fun and excitement.

The true meaning of the word recreation is re-creation and what better way to re-create oneself after hard labor in the fields or a stressful day at school than sitting in the shade beside the water, and experiencing the exhilaration of catching a fish.

I believe that Momma's fond recollections of fishing reveal a lot as to why she was not embittered by a harsh childhood. She had sweet memories of these and other moments of re-creation that she was able to use to temper the bitter realities of life. Beyond that, she would not let even the most severe of circumstances destroy her excitement and quest for meaning in life. I firmly believe that Lisa is filled with that same spirit and I rejoice as I observe it in her.

Tragedy was no stranger in Momma's girlhood home. She was just eight years old when news came that her half-brother, Nelson, who had left home to work on the railroad in Montana had been killed at work. He was twenty-seven. She had strong memories of the family grief over Nelson's death and especially remembered her Papa walking the floor, crying, and calling out his son's name over and over.

Every time I read the Biblical story of the death of Absalom or hear a sermon about it and picture King David tearing his clothes and crying out, "Absalom, Absalom, oh my son, Absalom," I think of Momma's description of her Papa as he cried out, "Nelson, Nelson," as he grieved the loss of his beloved son.

One of the tasks given to children in a large family is the care of younger family members. Momma quickly became the responsible big sister to her baby brother, Guy, who was born when she was seven. When she was twelve and Guy was five, he was accidentally shot in the stomach when one of his older brothers was attempting to dislodge a jammed bullet from his rifle and the rifle fired. Instead of rushing the child to the emergency room, as we would do today, Guy was nursed and cared for at home until, a few days later, it was unmistakable that his life was in grave danger. By the time a doctor was summoned from Hinton, peritonitis had taken its toll and he died.

As long as Momma lived, she would cry any time she recounted that terrible experience. She would recall how the little boy had asked his mother over and over again, "Momma, am I going to die?" The tragedy was compounded by the fact that Guy had been born into a very large and busy family and, after his tragic death, his parents realized that they had not given him the attention that he deserved.

Momma told of her mother's anguish in regretting that he had not been taken to church regularly because he did not have appropriate clothes; he still was primarily wearing children's "dresses" which were common for children of both sexes at that time. There were no pictures of him, so a photographer was engaged to take a picture of him laid out in death and artistically alter the picture to make it appear that his eyes were open. As you might imagine, this was an unusual and emotion laden picture.

Momma inherited that picture which, for some reason, she hung in my sister, Rhodetta's, bedroom, an honor that Rhodetta never did fully appreciate.

Maybe these terrible events somehow helped prepare Mom for other tragedies which she would have to face. I saw her faith and strength as she endured the heartache that came from seeing her two oldest sons go to war during World War II. Much later, I saw her face the untimely deaths of these same two sons. Shortly before the death of her son, James, she gave me more insight into the depth of other tragedies in her life.

James was terminally ill in a hospital in Richmond, Virginia, and Dad was already at the hospital with him, so when Rose and I came, we took Momma with us for what turned out to be her last visit with him. As we were driving past the Interstate 64 exit for Clifton Forge, Virginia, Momma pointed out the direction to a cemetery where she and Dad had buried a child. She described the baby boy as perfect and beautiful, but he was born with the umbilical cord wrapped around his neck and could not be revived.

I told her that I was aware that she had suffered a miscarriage or two before Arthur Jr. was born but I had not known about the full-term birth nor had I ever stopped to think of the trauma that they must have gone through. She then told us that she once thought that she would never have any children since, during the first five years of her marriage, she became pregnant every year but each pregnancy resulted in either a miscarriage or a stillbirth.

Momma was raised in a very strict, pious, religious home. Her Papa was the Rev. George Washington Meador, whose ancestry went back to Thomas Meador who came to the United States from England in 1636. George's great grandfather, or as he was described to me, "your granddaddy's great granddaddy," was the legendary Josiah Meador, Jr., who served in the Revolutionary War under the command of Gen. George Rogers Clark and whose last assignment was with the army at Yorktown in charge of British prisoners.

After the war, Josiah settled in Summers County, married Judith Lilly, felt called of God to preach, and established one of the first churches in the area, the Bluestone Baptist Church.

Due to the fact that the common Meador, Meadors, and Meadows surnames were used interchangeably at that time, and that Josiah "married into" the Lillys, one of the most populous families in the region, it was not a coincidence that my grandfather was commonly known as "Uncle George." He was probably related to a significant percentage of the people living in the Summers-Raleigh County area.

This intertwining of the families of southern West Virginia was borne out by a full-page article I was flabbergasted to see twenty years or so ago, in the Syracuse Post-Standard. This was a reprint from the Dallas Times-Herald with a dateline from Hinton, West Virginia. The article was all about the claim that was the subject of a case in the federal court claiming that members of the Meador family were the rightful owners of the rich Spindletop oil fields of Texas.

When word got out that an old relative named Meadors was listed on an old deed in Beaumont, Texas, for one-eighth interest in Spindletop, thousands of people named Meador, Meadors, Meadows, and Lilly, as well as those whose ancestor's had married anyone by those names, began lining up at the courthouses in Hinton and Beckley to get the needed documentation to prove their rightful claim on the promised billions of dollars. I have not gotten any money from the family lawsuit yet, and I suspect that I probably won't. The distant cousin who spearheaded the case has long since stopped writing and asking for money to cover the legal fees.

In addition to being a "slave driver" relative to the work on the farm, Grandpa set and enforced very high standards for morality and conduct. The latest in a line of preachers, his belief in the necessity of living a holy life led him to change from being a Baptist, which had been the family tradition, to the stricter, more pious Methodist denomination. His concept of holiness covered the whole spectrum of religious "don'ts," which forbade drinking, smoking, dancing, card playing, "immodest" dress, makeup, jewelry, or doing anything for pleasure on Sunday.

He even had a teaching on "idle words" which not only forbade the use of swear words or obscene language, but which also frowned even the use of inane expressions like "by the way," or "shucks," and he believed that "gosh" and "gee whiz" were just shortcuts to taking the Lord's name in vain.

He was so strict that Momma said that one joke she and her brothers and sisters would whisper to each other and laugh about was the one about the little girl who climbed up onto the rail fence and stared into the long, somber face of the family mule, and then commented, "You must be a Christian, because you look just like Papa."

From all indications, her Papa carried his piety to the extreme, maybe to the detriment of his family. All of his children were delivered by a midwife because he would not permit a male doctor look at his wife's body. Although that sounds ridiculously severe by today's standards, his insistence on this was not uncommon then, and maybe was the general rule.

Of my grandfather's children that I knew, only two of them lived by his strict standards, Momma and Uncle Azel. Fortunately, Momma's strictness was tempered and humanized by the warmth and love she was taught by her mother. Uncle Azel, though, seemed to be a near replica of his Papa.

One of Azel's neighbors in Hinton was Clyde Dillon, the most prominent politician in Summers County. As with most politicians, Sheriff Dillon, as he was known, was suspected to have a few character flaws. However, it was his son, Fred, who became a well known evangelist and pastor, rather than one of my cousins. Fred Dillon told Momma that, when he was a boy, he would ten times rather have his own father catch him smoking or swearing than for Azel Meador to catch him. I have always considered that this little story sheds some light on the reaction of the majority of Momma's siblings to their Papa's strictness and uncompromising rules.

"Uncle George is the preacher, but Aunt Rhody is the saint," was an often quoted description of Momma's parents. Rhoda Jane Crotty's great grandfather, Michael Crotty had emigrated from Ireland in 1813, and by 1837 he had settled in Monroe County. Her father, Jonas, was married to Elizabeth who was one-half American Indian. Momma had fond memories of her "Indian" grandmother, who she described as being small and dark, and a pipe smoker.

"Aunt Rhody" was known far and wide for her love and generosity. Her life was not an easy one. Momma said that her mother certainly did not have any idea of what her future was going to be on that day when she was so impressed by the handsome new preacher on his black horse. Married as a teenager to a stern, dictatorial older husband, instant stepmother to five boys, and then delivering a child every two years for over twenty years, she died at age fifty-six.

When Momma had her fifty-sixth birthday, it had a profound effect on her. "When my Momma died," she said, "I thought she was so old, but now that I am the same age as she was when she died, I realize that she was not old at all. She was just worn out."

One thing that made a strong impression on my Dad about Rhoda Jane, his mother-in-law, was something she told him before she died. She told him that she had prayed that each one of her children, now scattered all over the country, would be saved and that they would someday be united around God's throne, and that she firmly believed that God would answer her prayer. Although the lives of her children were very different from each other, and many found God in settings different than their strict upbringing, Dad once said that he had no doubt that the faithful prayers of that Godly woman were answered, in full.

So, who was Momma? She was a humble, faithful, generous, compassionate, loving person who sought to serve God and do his will every day, through Bible study, prayer, praise, and service to others. She gave no thought to hard work or hard times. I never saw her commit a selfish act or express a selfish thought. She was the most Christ-like example that I have observed in my entire life.

Where did she come from? The easy answer is that she came from hardy pioneer stock who shaped her life and destiny. But that is not enough of an answer. Although she was shaped by her ancestry and rigid upbringing, she was more, much more than that could have produced.

To me, and to everyone who knew her, she was a gift from God.

3

LOVE YOUR NEIGHBOR AS YOURSELF, OR "WHAT HAPPENED TO MY ROOSTER?"

"There is something so different in a gift which is born of <u>Love</u>! <u>God</u> gave to man the richest treasure of Heaven. He gave because He <u>Loved</u>. Shall we not at least give Him back our lives?"
Momma's diary: inside cover, undated.
Capitalized and underlined as written.

Reba and Clarence were our neighbors, living with their children, Ronald, Lillian, and Jimmy, at the Boyd place a mile and a half up the hollow behind our barn. They were the only people living up that hollow and their only access was a crude road, little more than a path, that led from our house to theirs. The road shared the narrow valley with a creek that snaked down the hollow, fueled by the runoff from some of the highest mountains in Summers County.

The creek criss-crossed over the road nine times in the mile and a half, which was no trouble in dry weather but when heavy rains or snow melts occurred, the little creek became a roaring torrent, sometimes covering the little valley.

Reba and Clarence just could not escape their economic woes. In a time when none of us had much, it seemed their lot in life to have even less. Reba had a lively wit and, due to her love of books, was educated well beyond that provided by her time in school, but she was frail and fragile. Job opportunities for Clarence were limited to things he could walk to, primarily farm labor and timber cutting in the general area and these jobs did not pay much and often there was no work at all during the winter.

As a child, I loved to go to their house. Their oldest son, Ronald, was my best friend. We spent virtually every Sunday together after church, either at my home or his, and sometimes both. A mile and a half is not very far for two energetic boys in a foot race.

Sunday dinner at our house was always a feast. I have a future chapter rolling around in my head about those Sundays, which will tell about Momma working all day Saturday so we could eat all day Sunday. So when Ronald and I ate at our house, it was a feast. At his house, however, sometimes it was a feast and sometimes it was not. One Sunday I clearly recall, Reba apologized profusely that all they had for dinner was mashed potatoes with uncolored margarine. Undaunted, Clarence said the blessing and then announced that "if money is the root of all evil, then we must be just about perfect." The laughter and good spirit there in the home went a long way in compensating for the lack of variety on the table that day.

Momma and Dad were usually aware of situations when there was specific need and provided some help. Dad decided to rent some pasture from the owners of the Boyd place and then made sure that he included a gentle cow in the small herd he located there which Reba could milk. Clarence was always the first choice when an extra hand was needed on our farm. Momma was less subtle and shared generously from her well filled storehouse of canned, dried, or cured foodstuffs whenever she was aware of a need. She always made a special effort at Christmas time to share her homemade candy, fruitcakes, and other goodies with them.

One Christmas season followed a particularly bleak year for Clarence. Momma intercepted him as he walked by our house on his way home a few days before Christmas. She inquired as to whether he was prepared for the holidays and found out that they did not have any meat for their Christmas dinner.

That evening at supper, Momma suggested that we should give one of our fat hens to Clarence for their Christmas dinner, but Dad balked at the idea. Momma kept and cared for about thirty hens and a rooster in our little chicken house. The hens kept the family in eggs and provided a few dozen for Dad to take to the Mick-or-Mack store in Alderson to trade for the groceries that we needed. The rooster assured that, in the Spring when some of the hens would brood and Momma would "set" the hens, their eggs would be fertile and hatch, thereby providing replacement hens to keep the egg supply going and providing some tasty young roosters for fried chicken. The rooster also was a very reliable alarm clock.

So Dad said "no" to Momma's recommendation that we give Clarence a hen in the spirit of Christmas, and she would not think of going against his decision. But after Christmas, it slowly began to dawn on Dad that something was missing. After three or four mornings of awaking in silence he suddenly asked, "What happened to my rooster?"

Momma's answer was prompt and honest, but not without a little bit of smug satisfaction. She had been faithful to Dad's decision to not part with one of our precious hens but, on Christmas Eve, she had again stopped Clarence on his way home and gave him the rooster for Christmas dinner.

The next Spring, since the eggs were infertile, brooding hens had to be placed in a coop until their brooding period was over and Dad had to buy a box of baby chickens from the Farmer's Equipment and Supply Store in Alderson.

I got a Valentine from Reba, Clarence, and Lillian, and one from Jimmy. I appreciate them remembering me. "
Momma's diary: February 7, 1958
(At least ten years after the Christmas rooster)

We had some truly great neighbors in our community and in many ways our lives were intertwined. When Ivan Mann had to have surgery, the men of the neighborhood got together and tended to his crops. When we were burning the brush from a "new ground" that we had just cleared, the wind came up and the fire got out of hand. In a short time, we were joined by neighbors who stayed with us, fighting fire, until it was under control.

Some activities involved the entire neighborhood. Every farm had a few acres of grain (wheat, oats, barley) which was cut by cradles wielded by the farmer and usually, a neighbor or two, and the cut grain dropped neatly in a row for the other workers to gather and bind it into sheaves. A cradle is a large implement somewhat like a scythe with a handle and a long blade, but unlike a scythe, the cradle looks like a giant hand with a series of long wooden "fingers" which "cradle," or catch, the cut grain to permit the grain to be laid out in an orderly row for the sheaf binders.

There were two methods used by the cradlers to get the grain from the cradle to the ground. Dad was a "gripper," in that after he cut a swath of grain with a wide swing of the cradle he released his left hand from the handle letting the cradle swing like a pendulum as he, in one swift motion, gripped the grain and dropped it immediately in the previous row of grain that had been mown. He then re-grasped the handle as it was still in motion and repeated the process.

Others swore that they could make better time by unloading their cradle by dropping the grain with an exaggerated swing of the cradle which brought the blade and fingers into a vertical position for a split second. Either way, cradling grain was an art. It was delightful to watch as three or four cradlers would work their way across a field or up a hillside, with the fastest on the left, then the next fastest, and so on, changing the field from one of golden grain being blown by the breezes into a field of stubble with perfect rows of mown grain waiting to be bound.

Binding, or tying, the grain was a job that was taught even to the youngest of the children. By the age of six or seven, I had learned how to gather the right amount of grain to form a sheaf and then select a small portion of the longer grain to use as a binder to tie the sheaf to hold it together. I had to pull the binder tight around a sheaf or bundle of grain and then twist the ends and, using the thumbs, tuck the ends securely back under the binder.

If this sounds slow and laborious, that is exactly the way I found it. The goal which Dad set before me was to be able to bind as fast as one man could cradle, a goal which I found to be unattainable. Momma, however, could bind as fast as any two men could cradle, sometimes with enough time left over to help me keep up.

After the grain was cradled and bound, it had to be shocked. Shocks were formed by grouping six or more sheaves, standing them on end so the grain heads were at the top, and then flattening and fanning out two "cap sheaves" and placing them on the top to shed the rain. Sometimes we stacked the sheaves around a pole, laying at least two rows of sheaves on their sides around and around the pole, with the grain heads inside the stack, first swelling the stack and then tapering it until a giant pear-shaped grain stack was formed and "topped out" with some hay to shed the rain.

The big neighborhood day came when the threshing machine

arrived. Frank Gore was the person in our area who had a threshing machine and a tractor which he used to pull the thresher from farm to farm and then to power the thresher. The thresher would be set up at the most convenient location, and the place would become a beehive of activity. John and Nell, our team of horses would be in harness, pulling our wagon as shock after shock of grain would be loaded by my brothers and hauled to the thresher. Neighbors would have brought their teams and wagons and would also be loading and hauling. The tractor would be put into place, the belt put on between the tractor and the thresher and the big, noisy, rickety machine would come to life.

Two people on the loaded wagon would start throwing sheaves onto the table of the thresher where two other people were standing with hawk-billed knives which they used to cut the binding straws and then they fed the grain, heads first, into the thresher. In just a matter of minutes, two products began to emerge from the machine. On the side of the thresher there were two openings through which the threshed grain passed. There were two or three people here to attach the sacks to the openings, trip the switch when one sack was full to the other opening, remove the full sack, tie it, load it into a wagon for transport to the granary, and attach a sack to the other opening before the next sack is filled.

The second product was the straw which came out on a conveyer belt or chain at the far end of the thresher. There a group of people with pitchforks worked endlessly moving the steady stream of straw, placing and tamping it around two poles forming an oval shaped straw rick.

An undertaking of this magnitude required a lot of support activity. My job, as a youngster, was keeping the water jugs full. When the grain fields were close to the house or a good spring, that was an easy task, but sometimes, when the distance was great, I could hear them yelling, "water-boy," long before I could get there.

And, of course, they had to eat and this was just as complex an undertaking as the threshing, itself. Typically, Momma would feed them in three shifts of eight, which was the capacity of her dining room table. Mountains of fried chicken, roast beef, mashed potatoes, brown beans, fresh vegetables, tomatoes, onions, corn bread, biscuits, cakes and pies would be consumed. Leora and Rhodetta would help with the serving and nonstop dishwashing required to accommodate such a large group. Often, one or more of the neighbor women would be there to help, but not if the threshing crew was due to be at her house the next day. If that was the case, she would be home cooking.

After the job was completed at our farm, Frank would hook the thresher to his tractor and head for the next location, the neighbors would return home, and we would organize our activities for the next week or two so we could return the favor to our neighbors by helping them as they had helped us.

Here I want to interject a story about the owner of the threshing machine, Frank Gore. The first thing that I remember hearing about him was Dad saying that "Frank Gore has the wickedest mouth of anybody I know." Frank could not talk without turning the air blue with his swearing and otherwise bad language. Of course, he toned it down around Momma, out of respect, but she knew of his "wickedness" and made it a matter of prayer.

The first breakthrough came one evening when Frank's son, Silas, came to our house to talk to Dad and Momma about something very important. Silas told them that he was certain that God was calling him into the ministry and he needed their advice since he only had a sixth grade education and had a family to support. I do not remember the exact words that Dad and Momma used, but they assured Silas that if he was sure that God was calling him, he must follow the call and trust God to provide.

He did follow the call and God did provide. Silas was soon in great demand to speak, due in no small part to who he was and people's natural curiosity to see what kind of a preacher Frank Gore's boy turned out to be. He turned out just fine and served faithfully as pastor of many rural churches during his lifetime.

The second breakthrough, or answer to Momma's and others' prayers, was the conversion of Frank Gore. It occurred one night during revival services at the Clayton Baptist Church. Our former pastor, Earl Ward, who was now the pastor of the Rollynsburg Baptist Church at Talcott, was the preacher. When the invitation was given, there was almost a congregational gasp as we all saw Frank Gore, in his work shoes, bib overalls and flannel shirt, walk down the aisle to surrender his life to the Lord.

Frank had no sooner gotten right with the Lord until he created a quandary for Brother Ward. Frank told the preacher that he wanted to be baptized "right now" and he was not going to go home until that was accomplished. Brother Ward explained to Frank that, since the "baptismal pool" was the swimming hole in the creek in the bottom of the valley below the church and that a baptismal service for all the converts was already scheduled for Sunday afternoon, maybe he should just wait until then. Besides that, Brother Ward reminded him, it was after ten o'clock and pitch dark outside.

But Frank was undeterred. So after a few cars were positioned so their headlights provided enough light to see the steep path down to the creek and illuminate the swimming hole, Brother Ward in his best suit and Frank Gore in his bib overalls waded into the creek and Frank was baptized "in the name of the Father, Son, and Holy Ghost," and Frank Gore was "raised to a new life in Christ."

Sometimes being a neighbor was tough duty. I found the following poignant entry in Momma's writings, dated December 25, 1953:

"Dad, Leora, and I went up to Burdettes awhile to be present when they told Nettie about Orvis."

The Burdettes lived just above the Griffith Creek Church and were wonderful neighbors but the visit this Christmas was not an easy one. When we were listening to the radio that morning we heard the worst possible news; Nettie's son, Orvis, had killed his wife and other members of her family and had then taken his own life. Upon hearing the news Dad became hysterical, yelling, "No! No! No! It can't be! Oh, Lord, it can't be!"

Momma was, as always in a crisis, calmer than Dad and she did not hesitate. She immediately began preparing to go be with her friend and neighbor in this terrible time of need. Momma went and did the tough duty and then entered just a single line about it in her account of Christmas that year.

Momma's diary is full of one line descriptions of her visits to her neighbors. She frequently mentioned visiting Ethel, a widow who lived nearby. She also mentioned visiting the Bowyers. Mr. Bowyer was an invalid who could no longer come to church so Momma helped to bring church to him. Not only did she visit them herself, she helped arrange for prayer meetings in the Bowyer home from time to time. She and

Dad took the pastor to the home so Mr. Bowyer could receive the Lord's Supper.

Tom and Nora Knapp lived at the end of the Griffith Creek road at the "head of the hollow," virtually in the shadow of Keeney's Knob which is the highest point in Summers County. When I was about six years old, there was nothing that I dreaded more than hearing that we were going to "see about" the Knapps. Mr. Knapp had a terribly painful arthritic condition in his back and lived in such a remote location that it was difficult to get him to a doctor or for a doctor to get to him. We would drive as far up the hollow as the car would go and then we would walk the rest of the way to their house. Long before we could see the house, we would hear Mr. Knapp screaming in pain.

As soon as Dad got ownership of his mother's little home and farm which adjoined our place, he and Momma immediately resolved to "bring the Knapps down out of the hollow" and into Grandma's house. And they did. Mr. Knapp eventually recovered sufficiently to resume his normal activities of gardening and selling vegetables to his customers in Alderson. Their new location and our car made it possible for them to become active in church. When my brother James came home from World War II and became the owner of "Grandma's place," (more about this later) the Knapps were able to become live-in caretakers of a nearby vacation home.

Then, when James and and his wife, Mary, were able to buy a larger farm, Dad and Momma again bought "Grandma's place." When asked if they were going to move into the now thoroughly modern house that James had remodeled, my parents' answer was, "No! We are going to bring the Knapps back home." And they did. Sweeter people than Tom and Nora Knapp never lived. They were like our family as long as they lived and they became the grandparents that I never had.

The little general store in our community was run by the Neely family. After the death of Mr. Neely, the store was the responsibility of Mrs. Neely and her son, Shelby. When Shelby was drafted into the navy during World War II the store was then operated by two strong and brave women, Mrs. Neely and Shelby's wife, Frances.

Dad worked part-time for the U. S. Department of Agriculture during the war, checking acreages of crops as part of some of the Roosevelt New Deal programs. Because of this job, Dad was entitled to different gas rationing classification and was one of the few people in our community who had a big enough government stamp on the windshield of his Model-A Ford to get to our big city, Hinton, on a regular basis. Being the good neighbor that he was, Dad always checked with people to see if there was anything that he could bring anyone from Hinton each time he went there.

A few days before Easter, in 1944, as he left for Hinton, Dad stopped at Neely's store to see if they needed anything. "Yes," Mrs. Neely said, "I need a new hat to wear to church on Easter."

"I beg your humble pardon, ma'am," Dad responded, "I thought that I would do anything in the world for you, but you have asked me to do the impossible. I am *not* going to pick out an Easter hat for you. That's just out of the question."

"Then I won't be in your Sunday School class on Sunday," Mrs. Neely told him. That was all it took. She got her hat and she wore it to church, proudly, that Easter Sunday.

To Momma, neighbor was an encompassing term and she never turned anyone away who was in need of anything. Although I came along late in the Great Depression, I still saw a number of people stop at our house looking for a handout, and they always got one. The ultimate example had occurred before I was born, when, during the height of the Depression a beggar and his big dog came to our house in the late afternoon looking for food. Momma invited him to join the family for supper and she even relented when he insisted that he bring his dog into the house and he fed the dog as he ate.

I still have a hard time believing this story, because, as long as Momma lived, I never saw an animal in her house unless it was a baby pig or lamb in need of warmth or medical attention in order to live. Momma's clean house was definitely off limits to pets.

But the story is not over yet. It gets worse. Night came and the man and his dog had not left. Bedtime came and they were still there. Momma's solution to that dilemma was to take Dad upstairs and give their downstairs bedroom to the man and his dog. The price she paid was having to salvage her bed the next day after it had been slept in by a very dirty man and his filthy dog. Dirt, odor, fleas, and bedbugs were the earthly rewards she received for her heavenly acts of kindness, but despite this, she never questioned whether she had done the right thing.

When I was a little boy, she often told me a story which

eloquently explained the way in which she viewed strangers. It was much later that I found out that her story was not from the Bible but was from Greek mythology, but that had not stopped Momma from telling a great illustrative story; she had just substituted Jesus for Zeus.

In Momma's version of the story, Jesus had made it known that he would be coming to a village on a certain day and would visit one home there. Everyone in the village made elaborate preparation in the hope that Jesus would select their home for the great honor of his presence. The people of the village watched and waited all day for Jesus to come but he never came.

The only person who came into the village that day was a poor beggar in tattered clothing who limped slowly up to every house and asked for something to eat. At house after house the beggar was treated rudely and chased away because the people were expecting a visit from Jesus and they did not want him to come and see such an unsavory character at their house.

The beggar proceeded through the entire village until he came to the last house where a poor widow lived. When the woman saw the beggar, she invited him to come in and, without hesitation, she spread out before him the food that she had prepared.

The beggar asked her how it was that she, a poor woman, could feed him so sumptuously. She replied that this was the day that Jesus was coming to the village and that she had spent all that she had in order to prepare a meal for him in the hope that he would choose her house to visit. She told the beggar that it looked like Jesus was not coming to her house and that it was obvious that the beggar was in great need of food so she was glad that she had the food to give to him.

Then, before the beggar began to eat, he bowed his head and gave thanks for the food and she immediately recognized that the beggar was actually Jesus. Jesus had chosen her house because she had been the one who showed compassion to him in the form of a beggar.

Momma didn't just tell that story, she lived it, even if the "could be Jesus" had a smelly dog, fleas, and bedbugs. We entertained preachers, neighbors, relatives, friends, and strangers.

We found out later that one of the strangers who stayed in our home overnight was actually an escaped criminal. I do not know if we were in any danger but, if we were, we were unaware of it. What I do know is that the criminal was treated with respect, fed a great supper, and got to hear Momma read a passage from the Bible and pray, thanking God for the one who was visiting us, before he went to bed.

She was a soft touch and everyone knew it. We never locked the doors of our house and sometimes, even if we were not there, people would feel free to make themselves at home.

When Earl Ward was the pastor of our little country church, he came from his home in Sandstone one weekend a month and preached on Saturday night, stayed overnight with us, and preached again on Sunday morning.

After one particularly long Saturday night sermon we arrived home rather late, so we just had a little refreshment, and then Brother Ward led our family devotions and headed upstairs to bed carrying a small kerosene lamp and a slop jar (chamber pot). In a few seconds he came to the top of the stairs and called out, "Sister Dodd, , , Sister Dodd, , , I believe there is somebody already in the bed."

"Oh," Momma said, "that's probably one of the Boyd boys. Just scoot him over and get in the bed with him."

Momma was right. It was Scott Boyd, a teenager who lived, appropriately, at the Boyd place. (This was before the Boyds moved to Charleston and rented the house to Reba and Clarence.) It was not unusual for Scott or either of his brothers, Richard or Tommy, to be tired out from their Saturday night in Alderson and the three mile walk to our house and just stop and crawl into one of our beds rather than walking the additional mile and a half on to their house. The fact that no one was at home did not matter.

Scott never did it again, though. He may have been somewhat traumatized by waking up in the middle of the night and finding three hundred pounds of preacher in bed with him.

As soon as my brothers and sisters left home, Momma had the space to do something she had always wanted to do; prepare a "prophet's room" like the woman in the Old Testament did for Elisha. So the front bedroom upstairs was freshly painted, new curtains were made and hung, and the newest and best of Momma's quilts placed on the bed so it would be ready for pastors, evangelists, singing school instructors, Bible School leaders, and anyone else who came to assist our church.

Caring for the "prophet" was not a small undertaking because revival meetings ran for a minimum of two weeks, and longer if "the

Holy Spirit was moving." Singing schools also lasted two weeks, as did Bible Schools, so Momma's "prophet's room" got lots of use. Of course, providing the room for the "prophet" was just the beginning. "Prophets" had to eat, bathe, and otherwise live so there was the added load of cooking, cleaning, laundering, and otherwise sharing living space with the "prophets" for protracted periods.

Although she never complained and tried to follow the Biblical admonition to "not become weary in well doing," Momma's unselfish, never ending concern for others rather than for herself eventually took a toll. More about this in a later chapter.

I want to conclude this chapter on neighbors, with a remarkable story, not about my Momma but about neighborhood mothers very much like my own. I am indebted to Junior Eggleston for this story.

Roy Snyder was a neighbor who was twelve years or so older than me. I remember Roy as a serious and studious young man. As a teenager, he was the clerk of our Sunday School, keeping all of the records and giving a report at the conclusion of Sunday School each week. He was raised in a humble family with a sweet, gentle mother and a stern father who was renowned for his ability to "squeeze a nickel."

The Snyder family suffered a great tragedy when Roy's brother, Leland, was killed in the battle of Iwo Jima during World War II. After the war, Roy and his brother, Jack, left for college and both had distinguished careers in academia, gaining their doctorate degrees and becoming college professors.

Now, this is where Junior Eggleston comes into the story. A few years ago, out of the blue, Junior heard a noise in front of his home in Covington, Virginia, and looked out to see his boyhood friend, Roy, now a professor at Ohio State University, getting out of an old, beat-up car. The car indicated that Roy had inherited at least one trait from his father.

Roy told Junior that he had come to see him because he was at the end of his rope. His wife was terribly ill and the strain of caring for her and anticipating her impending death was more than he could stand so, out of necessity, his doctor had told him he had to get away for a short time and try to gain the emotional strength that he needed to deal with the realities of his life.

He then asked if Junior's mother was still living, and if so, where did she live. When told that Mrs. Eggleston was well and living nearby right there in Covington, Roy said that he had an unusual request.

He told Junior that one of the things that he remembered most fondly and would give anything to experience again, was waking up to the familiar smells and tastes of his mother's breakfasts, and since his mother was dead, he had thought of Junior's mother.

"I can afford to stay at the Greenbrier and eat their breakfast," Roy said, "but they wouldn't know how to make biscuits and flour gravy like our mothers did. Would you ask your mother, that if I would pay her, could I spend a night at her house and then, in the morning would she make me a breakfast with biscuits and flour gravy?"

Junior's response was immediate: "I don't have to ask her, I know what her answer will be. No, you can't pay her, but I guarantee you that she would be the happiest person in the world to have you stay with her and let her fix breakfast for you."

So, Dr. Roy Snyder, eminent faculty member of Ohio State University, got his request granted. He was desperately searching for strength and he sought it in something that had been good in his life growing up as we did in a special place and time. He could not go back to being a boy, he could not find what he was looking for at his old home at Griffith Creek, and he could not visit his mother, but he was able to recapture something wonderful, nevertheless.

That great morning as he awoke to the smells of sausage frying, coffee perking, and biscuits baking, and walked into the kitchen as the flour gravy was bubbling in the black cast-iron skillet, even if the location was Covington, not Griffith Creek, and the woman in the kitchen was Nellie Eggleston instead of Gracie Snyder, he experienced a time of deep communion with his past, aided by the love of a sweet neighborhood mother from long ago.

And through his vivid memories, while familiar sounds, aromas, and tastes engulfed him, he gained strength as he communed with his own dear Momma.

4 MY GOD WILL SUPPLY ALL YOUR NEEDS, OR "JUST TURN THE CRANK"

"But my God will supply all your need according to his riches in glory by Christ Jesus." Philippians 4:19
A passage that guided Momma's life

When I was a child growing up, we never had much but it didn't seem to matter. Somehow we seemed to have everything we needed despite the fact that, by modern standards, we were somewhere between poverty stricken and "dead broke."

In the Spring of 1944, Dad's youngest brother, Larry, decided to sell the house and small farm that he had inherited from his mother and move his young family to Baltimore where he could work in a defense plant. This property joined our place so Dad borrowed the money to buy it for the modest sum of $2,400. Not $2,400 per acre, mind you, but $2,400 for the whole place, house, barn, and all. And then, less than a year later, he could not come up with the money to make the payments on the loan.

I remember walking down the road with him toward "Grandma's place," and, even though I was only six years old, being aware that he was terribly upset about something. When I asked him what was the matter, he told me that he did not have the money for a payment that was due at the bank and that he might lose the property which he had bought and was now farming.

Since I was the baby in the family, reasonably cute, and had lots of aunts and uncles, I had accumulated considerable wealth in a fat piggy bank. I had just recently been persuaded to do the patriotic thing and clean out the piggy bank and use $18.75 to buy a $25 War Bond.

My immediate reaction to learning of the reason for Dad's distress was to offer him my precious War Bond. I still remember how my offer miraculously changed his demeanor from dark to bright as he gently refused my offer and told me that he would find a way.

The "way" turned out to be an allotment check from my brother, James, who was in the Navy. When a service person's family had an income below a certain level, that service person could allot half of his pay to his family and the government would match it. So a small check started arriving each month and every penny of it went to pay off the loan. When James returned home after the war, "Grandma's place" became "James' place," as Dad transferred ownership to him, and this was where James began farming and where he and Mary, his bride, began their life together.

Dad never did anything the easy way. It seemed to me that anytime he arrived at one of life's forks in the road he always chose the one that was unpaved. Before he was married at the tender age of nineteen, he had taught school for a year in West Virginia and worked a year for the Firestone Tire and Rubber Company in Akron, Ohio, both of which were good jobs but he did not choose to stay with either of them.

He said that he chose not to continue teaching school because he did not like disciplining other people's kids. His career with Firestone was short lived because he missed his girl friend so much. I do not think that he considered marrying Momma and then living in Akron, and I do not know why. In the 1960's when Rose and I lived near Akron, we met many people in church who had, or whose family had, come to Akron from West Virginia, Kentucky, Tennessee, Missouri, and other southern states about the same time as Dad and had stayed for the rest of their lives.

After their wedding in 1918, Dad and Momma began their married life the hard way, living with Dad's parents and working on the farm where Dad was raised at Jumping Branch. Only four months had passed when they faced a crisis - Dad got a draft notice. He was called into the Army.

Dad told this story better that I could retell it, so I will let you hear it from him:

"It was November 11, 1918, and a bunch of us boys from

Summers County that had been called up were standing on the platform at the train station in Hinton, waiting to get on the train and leave for the army. Then a message came in over the telegraph saying that the Ar-**mis**-tice had been signed and the war was over and we could all go home. You never heard such whooping and hollering in all your life!"

I regret, big time, that I never asked Momma for her side of that story. All I can do now is speculate on the emotional roller coaster that she and Dad must have been on that day. First, there would have been a tearful separation of the young newlyweds, probably before day break, as Dad left for Hinton. And then the sadness and loneliness that must have engulfed Momma all that day as she faced the reality of living with her in-laws without her husband for who-knows-how-long, to say nothing of the fear that she may never see him again. After going through all of this, I can only imagine the excitement she experienced when, after hearing someone walk up onto the front porch that night after dark, the door opened, and there he stood. What a reunion that must have been.

Dad and Momma first set up housekeeping for themselves in Ronceverte when Dad got a promising job as a bookkeeper for the Chesapeake and Ohio railroad. Later, they moved to Clifton Forge, Virginia, when Dad's job was transferred there. Then they moved to Durban, West Virginia, where he took a job as a bookkeeper for a tannery. Shortly after Dad and Momma moved out on their own, Grandpa sold his big farm at Jumping Branch and bought a smaller one in the Griffith Creek community so his two youngest children could attend high school at nearby Alderson.

It was in Durban that their first child, Arthur Jr., was born in 1923. Their unbounded joy for at last having a beautiful and healthy child was quickly tempered by the news that Dad's father, James Lewis Dodd, was terminally ill with cancer. Grandpa died on June 1, 1924, and soon after, Dad and Momma bought the farm adjoining Grandma's, at Griffith Creek, so they could be close and help Dad's mother and his teenage sister, Gladys, and his little brother, Larry. On June 1, 1925, on the first anniversary of his grandfather's death, Momma's second son was born and was named James Lewis, after his grandfather.

Dad once told Rhodetta that he and Momma made a conscious decision to move to a farm because they believed that a farm was the best place to raise a family. I am thankful for that now, I guess, but there were many times that I seriously questioned that decision.

Life on the farm was tough, especially the way we did it. Most of our farm was steep and the little fields in the creek bottoms were very stony. The two small hilltop fields were virtually inaccessible. A few years ago, Rose and I drove my sisters and brother-in-law, Ralph Jones, to Durbin to see where Dad and Momma had lived in the early 1920's. As we drove there, passing large, beautiful farms in the wide valleys that Dad and Momma had passed through seventy years earlier, I kept remarking, "Why didn't they stop here and buy a farm," and, "look at that one there, why didn't they buy that one?"

I kept this up until Rose, rather pointedly, reminded me that if we had been raised there on one of those large beautiful farms, I would never have met her, so I quickly shut up about that subject.

What we actually had was commonly called a "general" farm, but it would more accurately be called a subsistence farm. In order to "subsist" we did all sorts of different things. We usually had a herd of a dozen cows or so, and we milked four or five of the tamest ones, ran the milk through a separator, and sold some of the cream at the creamery in Alderson. Momma churned the rest of the cream and made homemade butter, some of which she also sold when there was any demand for it. Dad sold the calves that arrived each year when they reached veal weight.

We always had at least one brood sow which meant that we had two litters of pigs each year which we sold at weaning time for as much as $10.00 apiece. We would keep three or four of the spring pigs each year, fatten them on home grown corn, butcher them in the fall, cure the meat, and, if there was a market, sell the best parts and eat the rest. Nothing went to waste. On butchering day we would feast on jowl (rhymes with bowl), which Momma would fry up nice and crisp and serve with biscuits and gravy. On succeeding days we would enjoy the ribs, backbone, pig's feet, hog head cheese or "souse", and fresh tenderloin.

The hogs were carefully cut into hams, shoulders, and bacons, and these prize cuts were laid on a wide shelf in the smokehouse and covered with a sugar-cure mix of brown sugar, salt, and pepper. All of the trimmings became sausage by being put through a hand turned meat grinder, seasoned with Momma's own blend of salt, pepper, sage, and other seasonings, and then shaped into patties, lightly fried, packed into half-gallon jars, covered with newly rendered, melted lard and sealed for future use. Not only were these canned morsels the best side dish ever created to go with buckwheat cakes in the morning, they were sometimes a delicious quick addition to a Sunday dinner when more people showed up than even Momma had prepared for on Saturday.

After the hams, bacons and shoulders had "taken the cure" or absorbed the mix, they were placed in individual white cloth sacks and hung in the smokehouse for long term use or for sale. The "country hams" were often in demand, but if they did not sell, they were the items that Momma was most likely to give to someone. I complained to her once that while other people were enjoying our ham, we were eating fatback.

Even the portions of the hogs that we did not use did not go to waste. We had friends who would come on butchering day and take the kidneys, lungs, and intestines. Momma drew the line on some things. Even though Dad sometimes reminisced out loud about how his mother had cleaned out the intestines and prepared "chitlins" that were "pretty good eatin'," Momma never took the hint.

"It has been a nice day. The water thawed out. Got 7 eggs. I saw two red foxes across the creek in front of the house. Cleaned the house and churned and wrote Paul. We had a good nights rest"
Momma's diary: January 10, 1958

Momma always had a few laying hens that she cared for which provided eggs to cook with and to sell at the Mick-or-Mack store. We rarely ate eggs for breakfast because they were one item that could always be sold. Each spring we had baby chickens, either purchased or hatched by our own brooding hens. The pullets were kept for replacement laying hens and the young roosters were either sold live, door-to-door in Alderson, or dressed, fried, and eaten.

One year Dad got scammed when he bought some bargain baby chickens. One Spring evening, after dark, a man stopped his truck at our house and asked Dad if we could use some baby chickens. He said that after his deliveries that day he had just one box of one hundred chicks left and he needed to get rid of them and that Dad could have them for only two dollars. Dad's first reaction was that, "at that price, they must be all roosters." "No," the man assured him, "they are 'hatchery run.' There will be the same number of pullets as there are roosters."

Dad then took his flashlight and looked at the baby chicks and when he saw that they were a pale yellow color he made his second profound observation: "Now I see why they are so cheap. Those chickens are White Leghorns and they never will get big enough to make good fryers."

"Oh no," the man said, "those are not White Leghorns, those are White Rocks and White Rocks are big chickens." He asked what kind of chickens we usually raised, and when Dad told him "Rhode Island Reds," the man scoffed and assured us that these White Rock chickens would get a lot bigger than our piddlin' little Rhode Island Reds.

Within a few weeks it became evident that our "White Rocks" were not going to get very big because they were, indeed, White Leghorns. The second shoe dropped as they got old enough for us to tell their sex and we found that we had one pullet and ninety-nine little skinny, puny roosters. Dad was livid and not one bit surprised when all of our regular customers took one look at our little roosters and chose not to buy any.

Momma was undaunted, though. She told Dad, who was impatient and did not want to hear it, to just wait a couple of weeks while the roosters grew a little more and they would be able to sell them. Two weeks later, Momma and I picked out about ten of the fattest (if you can ever call a White Leghorn fat) chickens, chopped off their heads, scalded them, and picked off the feathers.

She then carefully removed the insides of the chickens and we ended up with ten of the most beautiful little "roasters" you ever saw. Having been fed lots of corn, their skins were a golden yellow, and with their wings tucked under and the drumsticks drawn down, those chickens looked downright plump. Dad promptly sold all ten of them that week and more each following week to satisfied repeat customers until about ninety of the chickens were sold. I am not sure about the exact number sold but we undoubtedly ate at least nine of them.

We had as many as fifteen hives of honey bees which we robbed during the summer and usually we were able to sell some honey. Dad loved honey bees. One of his favorite Sunday afternoon activities was looking for "bee trees." If he could find bees "watering" at a remote location on the farm, this would tell him that there was a "bee tree" of wild bees in the vicinity and he would not rest until he had located it.

He would watch the bees fly off from their watering place and locate the "bee-line" toward a distant hollow tree. He would take a little flour in a paper bag and sprinkle some on the bees as they watered which would make them more visible as the sun glinted on their backs which would permit him to watch them a little farther on their journey toward their tree.

After he found the "bee tree," he would wait for just the right day and then we would take an empty "bee gum" (hive) that had been washed with apple leaves dipped in salt water (don't ask me why), an axe and a crosscut saw and go cut down the bee tree. We would then, after quieting the bees with lots of smoke, cut a large hole into the hollow tree and collect the honey. Next, the queen bee had to be located and placed or smoked into the prepared hive so the rest of the colony would move in with her.

Then we would go back that night and carry the new colony, in the dark, up hill and down being careful not to fall, until we got it home and placed on a platform along side Dad's other hives. He got some interesting bees this way.

One hive of wild bees he obtained in that way was particularly ornery. They even looked different; more black than yellow. One spring day when Dad was trying to corral and hive a swarm of them (swarming is how bee colonies reproduce) the entire swarm attacked him, covering him with thousands of angry bees stinging him through his clothing.

Fortunately, he was wearing a bee veil so his face and head were protected, but there was nothing he could do to get rid of the bees so he ran and jumped into the swimming hole below the waterfall in the creek in front of our house and then watched as that swarm of bees floated downstream. Even with his protective clothing and beekeeping garb, he suffered from dozens of stings.

As Dad got older, he let the number of bee hives dwindle down to two, which he kept until his death. His number of hives dwindled because he got to the point that he could no longer climb to the tops of the trees on the steep hillside behind his bee hives to capture the swarms which occurred each spring.

When a new queen bee hatched in a hive, the old queen had to depart and when she left, a portion of the hive's population went with her. When this occurred, we could hear the roar of the swarm even if we were inside the house and we immediately ran outside and began ringing cowbells or banging on metal objects which, we believed, encouraged the swarm to "settle."

The swarm "settled" when the queen would alight on a branch near the top of a nearby tree and the swarm would form a cluster around her about the size of a gallon jug and remain there until scout bees could locate a suitable hollow tree for the swarm to move into as a permanent residence. This provided a "window of opportunity" of thirty minutes or so for Dad to place an empty hive near the tree where the swarm was temporarily settled, and climb up the tree with a saw and rope, tie the rope to the limb holding the swarm, saw off the limb and lower it slowly to the ground, climb down the tree, and then entice or force the bees into the hive.

This became too difficult a task for a seventy-something year old man with arthritis, so he had to let most of his swarms get away, but not without a fight. He was particularly proud of one swarm he captured by using his twelve gauge shotgun to shoot the limb above a swarm and, after the cluster splattered on the ground, he was able to locate the queen and put her into the hive and the rest of the swarm followed.

I always knew that anytime I visited back home in the summertime Dad would have plans for me to help him "take off the honey." In his later years as Dad became frail, lifting and carrying the filled supers of honey was too much for him, and not just anybody will help you get that up-close and personal with bees.

Even if Dad had not seen us for six months, if the sun was shining, we would not be with him more than ten minutes until he would say, "You know, Son, it looks like an awful good day to take off some honey," and he would fire up the smoker, hand me the smelly remnants of what once was a bee veil, put on his nice, new bee veil, and away we would go.

On one such occasion a few years after Momma had died, when Dad was about eighty, we had removed a super of honey from the hive, relocated it to the back yard where we smoked the remaining bees away from the honey and were cutting the beautiful filled, capped white combs of sourwood honey from the wooden frames, and placing them in a large pan. My wife, Rose, my sister, Leora, and Dad's friend,

Evelyn, were there to assist in this part of the operation.

When I worked around bees, I took certain precautions, especially to assure that none of those smoke-drugged bees crawling around the yard would happen to wander up my leg. The way I did this was to simply tuck my trouser legs into my socks so the bee could not gain entry to my legs.

Old Dad was way too confident to do anything like that. He didn't worry about those little itty-bitty bees. That is, until he felt one, way up high on his leg. Dad only carried about a hundred and fifty pounds around on his six foot frame and his baggy legged trousers were probably two sizes too large, so the errant honey bee had crawled up the inside of his trouser leg until it had reached the point where trousers and Dad came together, and that is when he felt it.

"Whoa," he yelled. "I think I'm in trouble here. It's a-gonna ruin me. You women better get in the house because I am a-comin' out of these britches." As the women beat a hasty retreat he quickly dropped his trousers and, sure enough, there was that inebriated bee, perched precariously on Dad's bony behind.

We grew sorghum and made cane molasses which we sold for $2.50 to $3.00 a gallon in the 1940's. Molasses making was an all consuming job for a month to six weeks each fall. Not only did we squeeze the juice from our own crop and boil our own sorghum, people from a twenty-five mile radius would bring their sorghum cane to be squeezed and boiled. The first pan of juice would go on the fire at 5 o'clock in the morning and boil while the juice for the second pan of the day was being collected by running the cane stalks through a mill to squeeze out the juice which flowed into a large tub covered with a cheesecloth strainer.

The first pan would be finished before noon, the molasses removed, the pan refilled with juice, and the process would be repeated. The third pan of molasses would be finished about 11 o'clock at night, at which time the fire would be put out, the juice already extracted for the early morning pan would be covered, and we would go to bed so we could get up early the next morning and do it all over again.

This was my favorite time of the year. Molasses making was a social event for everybody but Dad and Momma. Neighbors would come by after supper and stay until the last pan "came off." Men and boys would search through our woodshed for just the right piece of wood and then, using their pocket knives, whittle thin wooden "paddles" with which they would scrape the pan for the sweet goodness clinging to the side of the pan after the molasses had been dipped out. Junior Eggleston, a teenager at that time, would often bring his guitar and the night air would be filled with music.

The pile of cane stalks, soft after their trip through the grinding mill, provided a great spot for children to roll, romp, wrestle, or play "king of the hill."

Momma was smarter that the rest of us, though. I cannot remember a time that she did not say that the work was too hard for what we got out of it. Sometime, before 1950, her wisdom was heeded and the molasses making came to a halt.

About thirty years later as Dad was sampling some molasses that Rhodetta had brought him, after he had made his inevitable comments about their inferior quality in comparison to the ones that he used to make, he asked her, "How much did you pay for these?"

"Six dollars," she replied. "Six dollars a gallon?" he asked. "No, Daddy," she said, "six dollars a quart.". "Six dollars a quart," he shouted in disbelief, "Why child, that's twenty-four dollars a gallon. Law have mercy, if I was just ten years younger I would plant this whole place to cane."

We grew our own buckwheat which we took to Blaker's Mill, an old water-powered stone mill near Alderson, to be ground into flour for our winter supply of buckwheat cakes.

I had a great surprise a few years ago when I was at the West Virginia State 4-H Camp at Jackson's Mill for a speaking engagement. Since we had arrived early, Rose and I had time to leisurely walk the grounds of that beautiful facility where I had spent some happy times as a teenager. Suddenly, I saw something that was, at the same time, both foreign and familiar. Foreign because there was something that had not been there when I had attended Future Farmer of America camps as a high school student, but familiar because I recognized it. "Rose," I said, "look at that old mill. I could swear that was Blaker's Mill from back home, but what is it doing here?"

As we got closer, we read the sign explaining that, although Jackson's Mill was named for the mill that Stonewall Jackson's family had operated on the site, that mill had been destroyed many years ago. Recently there had been a search for a similar mill in working condition which could be taken apart, piece by piece, and relocated at this site. That search had resulted in my old friend, Blaker's Mill, being selected and now it stood proudly in place of the historic Jackson's Mill.

We grew our own white Flint corn, some of which was ground into meal for cornbread and some of which we processed into hominy. We took our wheat to the mill at Alderson where it was ground into flour and we brought our portion home while the rest went to the mill as payment for the grinding. We also grew extra potatoes for sale, cranberry and yellow-eye beans, and, occasionally a small "patch" of pumpkins and winter squash to sell.

As I recount all of this, I realize that we had an abundance of everything but money. I assure you that we never went hungry. But I also remember times being so tough that we could not afford more from the grocery store than what we could pay for with money we got from the cream and eggs that we had to sell that week.

Momma's faith that the Lord would provide never wavered, even during our hardest times. Dad would sometimes get discouraged and exclaim, "Why does everything have to happen to me?" But Momma was a rock. She would soothe Dad and she always had an answer for us. One answer that she usually gave me when I needed or wanted something that we did not have was, "just turn the crank."

By this, she meant that I should use my head and my hands instead of just complaining. The remarkable thing about it was that, as I put my brain in gear and got involved in doing something about a need or problem, some solution was always found. I am sure that you know some "Plan A" people who demand one single solution to any problem and will not accept any alternative. Momma taught me to be not only a "Plan B" person, she taught me to be a "Plan C, D, or E," person.

I learned from her that there is always an answer but it may not be my first choice. Wonderfully, I discovered that the answer you have to work for, wait for, or seemingly settle for usually turns out to be infinitely better that "Plan A" would have been. She knew that God was in charge and that he had all of the answers but some of them did not come easy. She believed that God could move mountains but she was certain that he expected us to get our shovels and do some serious digging.

Momma never wasted anything nor did she throw anything away that she thought may be of some use to someone in the future. I have had a little difficulty over the past forty years adjusting to a wife whose philosophy seems to be, "if you're not using it, you're losing it!" When I am preparing to teach one of my college classes, I will remember a newspaper or magazine article that I have read during the last day or two and seek to retrieve it. I spend a lot of time going through the recyclable bin.

One day, a couple of years ago, Rose insisted that we go for a walk. My sneakers were getting pretty ragged so I went upstairs to my closet to get an old pair of soft soled leather shoes. When I could not find them and called down to Rose to ask if she knew where they were, she replied in an exasperated voice, "I don't believe this! Those old shoes were just collecting dust in the corner of your closet. You hadn't worn them for over a year so I took them yesterday and gave them to the Rescue Mission. You don't use them for a year but the very next day after I get rid of them, you decide you need them."

I moped around for days missing what now had become my favorite pair of shoes and I seriously considered going to all of the Rescue Mission outlet stores to see if I could find them, in the event they decided to sell them rather than give them to a needy person.

A few days after Dad's funeral, Rose and I, with Leora and Rhodetta, went to the home place to decide what to do with Momma's and Dad's belongings. We divided up the things that we wanted, decided what should be given away and to whom, and, finally, what should be destroyed. I was quickly delegated to the removal and burning of the latter.

Momma and Dad each had a closet in their bedroom. Dad's closet was near the bed and was just a curtained-off enclosed area that he had created by putting up a wall of two twelve inch boards from the floor to the ceiling and connecting it to the outside wall of the room with a five foot rod on which he hung his clothes. He had built in one large shelf above the rod where he put his hats, books, shotgun shells, and assorted other stuff.

Momma's closet was at the end of their bedroom, and it was the area under the stairway. The area was enclosed and was accessible through a small, hand made door which was kept shut by a simple piece of wood mounted beside the door which could be rotated across the edge of the door. The Christmas decorations and other seldom used things were stored in the part of her closet under the lower steps and her clothes hung where there was ample headroom.

Both closets were always full of clothes, although they rarely bought anything new. From the time Dad was fifty years old, when he would get a new suit, often at the insistence of his children or even as a gift from one of us, he would always say, quite seriously, "Well, that's all the suit I'll ever need. You can bury me in that suit." Of course, Dad's flair for the dramatic overstatement did not stop with clothing. Each of the last ten or so cars that he bought was always introduced to the family with, "This is all the car I'll ever need."

Their closets were full because they never got rid of anything. Keep stuff they had not worn in a year? They kept stuff that they had not worn in a decade. When their infrequent acquisition of anything new forced the removal of some old garment, it went to the corner of the enclosed back porch where Dad had put up a rod for hanging things. There was a large wooden box there that held more old clothes, and there was a curtain over this entire area. When the back porch got to be too cluttered, the next place, for the really old stuff, was a section of the smoke house, the building which was closest to the back porch.

They saved everything else, too. One of the things that was a challenge to dispose of was a keg full of bent, rusty nails that Dad had accumulated. Whenever he pulled out a nail, he saved it and had done so for sixty years. After considering a slim list of options, I dumped them down into the privy pit, before it was destroyed and the site leveled. I have to smile when I think that someday, somehow, someone with a metal detector will find that "hot spot" and be convinced that they have found the elusive "pot of gold" that was reportedly hidden somewhere on the property during the Civil War.

Can you imagine the consternation and puzzlement when they dig up the "buried treasure" and it turns out to be a keg of bent, rusty nails dropped into an abandoned toilet pit?

Old clothes, worn out shoes, bent nails, broken tools, cracked jars, leaky buckets, musty old books, and two desks full of old records, receipts, and correspondence faced me. Keeping a bonfire going for two days to get rid of the combustibles gave me a lot of time to think about my parents and their way of life, and everything that I was getting rid of was a reminder of them.

"Just turn the crank," Momma would say to me when I expressed a need for almost anything. No matter what was needed, we could usually find it. If a button was needed, first we would look into her big sewing basket, and if the right one was not found, there was an endless storehouse of buttons on old garments on the back porch or in the smoke house. I did not even have to ask what to do when I needed a shoelace, I just went to the pile of old shoes in the smokehouse and retrieved the best looking lace I could find.

So I learned from Momma that old clothes could be shared with the needy, they could be worn in an emergency, they could be "mined" for needed items like buttons or zippers, or they could be cut up and reused in crocheted rugs and patchwork quilts. Momma's patchwork quilts were an absolute necessity to keep us warm on cold winter nights in our drafty, uninsulated house. I remember sleeping under such a pile of quilts that I could not turn over in the bed. But I stayed warm.

To get one of Momma's newly crocheted rugs placed by your bed was an honor, indeed. Thick and soft, it was just the thing to keep your warm feet from touching the cold, hard floor when getting out of bed on a zero morning. When the rug began to get a little bit of wear and was replaced at the bedside by a new one, it was not thrown away. Oh no! It was relocated.

The first stop for the relocated rug would be just inside the doors coming into the living room and kitchen from outdoors, as secondary foot wiping or snow melting locations. When they became too dirty to be left in the house, they would then be placed outside those doors on the porches to serve as primary sites for foot wiping.

It probably would not surprise you if, at this point, I were to tell you that Momma believed in modesty. Shorts, short skirts, sleeveless dresses, even slacks were not what Momma considered proper attire, either for herself or for other women. Stay with me now, this does have a connection to crocheted rugs.

Momma's sister, Una, lived in Anderson, Indiana, and came each summer for a visit of a couple of weeks. During one of these visits, Momma and Aunt Una were sitting on the front porch when one of the older men of the neighborhood who was walking up the road, turned and began walking toward our house. Realizing that her voluptuous sister was wearing those "old shorts," Momma moved quickly to save the day. Before Mr. Gregory had reached the front steps, Momma grabbed the dirty, worn, old foot cleaning rug from the porch floor, slapped it down on Aunt Una's lap, and made sure that it stayed there until the neighbor left. There was just no end to the uses Momma could find for her rugs!

I also learned that a pile of old shoes could provide not only shoelaces, but it could provide replacement heels for the shoes I was wearing, it could provide an old shoe tongue which made a perfect stone holder for a gravel shooter or slingshot, and it could provide the piece of leather that Dad needed in order to splice together two pieces of the horse's harness that had come apart.

Bent nails could be straightened and reused, saving both money and a trip to town to the hardware store. Broken tools can serve purposes other than the one for which they were manufactured. They may serve as wedges, pry bars, or shims, depending on the size and shape of the tool. Cracked jars can no longer be used for canning, but they can still be used to dip water for watering flowers or seedling vegetables and they make good storage receptacles for paint brushes, washers, and screws. A bucket that will not hold water may be a very adequate container to use when feeding the chickens.

Musty old books? I had gotten an education from those musty old books. They were a motley collection of hand-me-down books, old school books, and books Dad bought at auction sales where he worked as a clerk. He did not intentionally buy the books at the auctions but when no one else would bid he would bid a quarter or fifty cents to get it started and sometimes that would be the only bid and he would get a box of books.

Through those books I became acquainted with Aesop, Gulliver, Robinson Crusoe, and Beowolf. I learned about the battles of the Trojan war, the conquests of Alexander the Great, the rise and fall of Rome, the discovery and settling of America, the Revolutionary War, the Civil War and World War I. I came to know authors like Homer, Hawthorne, Stevenson, and Defoe at an early age.

"My God will supply all of your needs," the Bible tells us, and Momma believed that and told us that very frequently. But she never sat down and waited on a miracle. She knew that God was faithful and would do his part but he expected us to do our part and that was why she would tell us to "turn the crank." Her life was a great testimony to the truth of the scriptures and to the wisdom of her philosophy.

Momma never failed to "turn the crank," and God never failed to supply her needs. They had a great partnership.

5 LOVE YOUR ENEMIES, OR
"I'D RATHER LICK HIM THAN EAT!"

"As far as I know, I do not have an enemy in the world. I have searched my heart and I am sure of one thing; I love everybody.
Momma's often repeated testimony

It always appeared to me that Momma really did love everybody. The only time I ever recall her referring to anyone as enemies was during World War II when we had some official ones, and the only time she used the term was when she was praying.

I have some clear memories of 1943, the year I turned five years old, because of some very significant happenings which occurred that year and etched themselves on my brain. I remember early that year when Mom got a postcard from her brother Claude saying that he had been assigned to Europe. Although Uncle Claude was thirty-eight years old, since he was not married he had been drafted into the Army. When Momma read his postcard, she started to cry. When I asked why she was crying, she said that she was afraid that we would never see Claude again because he was going to have to cross the ocean and fight the war.

And fight the war he did, from the Normandy Landing to the Battle of the Bulge to the liberation of the concentration camps. After the war he told us graphic stories of his experiences. Once when his unit had been defeated and the German soldiers were examining the American casualties and running their bayonets through the wounded who were still alive, Uncle Claude said that he laid very still, praying, as a German soldier stood over him, kicked him, and then said "heim kaput" (he's dead), and moved on.

He also recalled the indescribable horror of the concentration camps and how he and his fellow soldiers were greeted by the weeping, starving survivors who looked like walking skeletons. He told of liberating one camp where Russian soldiers were imprisoned and described how those who were strong enough used cans, combs, and other make-shift instruments to do a rendition of "The Stars and Stripes Forever" in honor of their American comrades. He was never the same after his war experiences. He lived to a ripe old age but was never free of the fears and paranoia that we believed were caused by the trauma of his war experiences.

On the first day of June, 1943, my brother James celebrated his eighteenth birthday and was immediately drafted into the Navy. James was a very shy boy who would never stay away from home overnight and would rarely even eat a meal at a friend's house. But Momma had to let him go, and after his basic training, he immediately faced the horrors of war by serving as a gunner on a Liberty ship, dodging German bombs and U-Boat torpedoes, making repeated trips across the Atlantic Ocean.

On his first trip across the Atlantic he was on the middle ship of a three ship convoy when torpedoes hit and sank the first ship and then the third ship. One of the ships was carrying oil and gasoline which spread over the surface of the ocean and caught fire, creating a blazing inferno as those on James' ship rescued as many of the survivors as possible. Momma and Dad both cried as they discussed the horror that their teenaged boy had to endure just weeks out of high school.

Then at the end of August, my oldest brother, Arthur Jr., graduated from college after three years and the 1943 summer session, and was immediately drafted into the Navy and sent into the war against Japan in the Pacific. This was Momma's first child, the one who suffered most terribly from a family malady, migraine headaches. Now he, disabling headaches and all, was in the Pacific Islands, taking reconnaissance photographs while floating in the air in a blimp, which seemed to his frightened parents to be the most vulnerable of targets.

Momma's prayer times got pretty long during the war. We always had prayer before going to bed and Momma was the one who prayed aloud. She always knelt, so I did likewise which permitted me to lay my head on the couch and take a nap if her prayers became too long. But I was awake most of the time and I recall her praying for "our precious boys, Junior and James," and "dear Claude," in addition to praying, by name, for all of the young men from our community who were in service, and for the families around us who had lost their sons in the war. She would also ask God to grant wisdom to "our President," and "our generals," and "all those in authority."

And then, she would say, "Lord, you have told us in your Word to pray for our enemies," and she would. Her prayer for her enemies would begin by being inclusive of all who were involved in the war and then she would pray specifically for those in combat on both sides. She would express her concerns for the mothers and fathers who were going through the heartache that she and Dad were experiencing and pray especially for those who had lost "their dear loved ones" in the fighting. She prayed for the Germans and Japanese knowing that the very persons she was praying for were the ones who could snuff out the lives of her beloved sons or brother.

This was at a time when the enemies of our country were being publicly depicted as evil, sadistic, depraved, inhuman forces unworthy of any feelings of sympathy, let alone love. The caricatures of them on posters, in the newspapers, and in the comics I was starting to read were hideous. Still, Momma prayed for them. Somehow she was able to see beyond the politics of this world, and even beyond the overwhelming feelings she had for her loved ones engaged in the battle, to see the world as God sees it and have compassion for everyone.

I thought about Momma during "Desert Storm," when the United States was able to quickly eliminate Iraq's threat to Kuwait and our country's oil interests. As a country, we watched the whole operation on television, seemingly with the same attitude that we have when we watch a football game. We were jubilant. Our side was winning. Not only were we eating up the yards and going toward their end zone, we were losing hardly any people and we were able to wipe out one hundred thousand of them. Wow! What a great day!

I am sure that Momma would not have been jubilant but, rather, would have been saddened by "Desert Storm." Not by the results, because the politics of the situation would not have been a big factor to her. She, like God, would have been saddened by the deaths of one hundred thousand young men and she would have been fully aware of the sadness in one hundred thousand homes, and she would have shared in the anguish of one hundred thousand mothers.

Momma was so full of love and the Holy Spirit that concepts that are next to impossible to most of us, things like "loving your enemies, turning the other cheek, and going an extra mile," were not just platitudes, they were an integral part of who she was. And not just once in a while, but always.

Dad approached the whole enemy thing a little differently than Momma did. He could hold a grudge longer than anyone I ever knew. He was living with Les and Leora at the time of his death and they said that on the way to the hospital on the day he died, he prayed aloud, asking God to forgive him for the harmful things that he had done to other people. He was a devout man of great faith but his natural inclination was born of a long line of hard-headed people, especially on his mother's side of the family.

Dad was a genuine mountain man. He loved the outdoors and hard work and was not afraid to tackle anything or anybody. He enjoyed all kinds of hunting and his overriding passion was coon hunting. This took place at night with the help of a good dog or two, a lantern, a strong flashlight, and a small rifle which he used to shoot the coon after the dogs had treed it. He was so good at it that he sometimes supplied all the meat for the annual Coon Hunter's Banquet, sponsored by the Hinton Chamber of Commerce.

Once, during the 1970's, I was able to attend a reunion of his Uncle John Dodd's descendents with him in Goldenrod, Florida. As he was going through the food line he stopped before a bowl of turkey meat and gravy and as he helped himself to a good-sized portion of it, he asked, "What is this in this bowl, anyway?"

"Why, Arthur," one of his Florida relatives told him, "that's armadillo," and then smiled as he watched Dad put most of it back into the bowl.

As soon as we sat down to eat, Dad asked me, quietly, "What is an armadillo?" I replied that it was sort of like a possum in a shell. He then cautiously took a small bite of his "armadillo" and said, "That don't taste too bad." "Yeah," I responded, "it tastes a lot like turkey, doesn't it?" Suddenly he realized that he had been "had" and turned to see that he had taken his first taste of "armadillo" to the great delight of his Florida relatives.

I did not let him off that easy. I told him that I was thoroughly ashamed of him. He had always hunted and shot anything that crept or crawled in West Virginia and expected Momma to cook it and us to eat it and now he was about to turn up his nose at another wild animal just because it lived in another part of the country. Even he had to laugh at this irony.

Dad was sometimes painfully blunt and could be a bit caustic, at times. One day during World War II, we had an unexpected visitor. As she walked toward our house from her car, without warning, our old crippled dog, Trixie, took a major chunk out of the ample calf of the stranger. As soon as she got into the house, Momma quickly gave her the best emergency treatment that soap, water, iodine and bandages could provide, and then we found out why the woman had come.

One of our neighbor's sons had been given an agricultural deferment, which meant that he was approved to stay at home and work on the farm rather than being drafted into active military duty, and our visitor was an investigator seeking to determine if the young man actually deserved the deferment.

It was quickly obvious that Dad did not like answering the woman's questions and he got even more agitated when she turned her attention to what he was going to do with his vicious dog. He explained to her that Trixie was his oldest son's dog and that all he was going to do was take the best care of that dog that he could "until my boy gets home from the war."

Junior's really loved this dog which was almost as old as he was. They had grown up together and had been inseparable for years on the farm. Once, when Junior was petting Trixie, he told me that when he died he hoped that he would go to dog heaven because he loved dogs so much. Don't ask me why he gave his boy dog the girl dog name, Trixie, but for some reason he did. Anyway, back to the story.

"But," the woman protested, "he is dangerous. You have to protect people from a dangerous animal like that."

"That dog never bit anybody before in his life," Dad told her, "and he is so gentle that every kid in the neighborhood plays with him."

"If he is so gentle and harmless," the woman persisted, "then why do you think he bit me?"

"Well, ma'am," Dad said, slowly and deliberately, "it may be that he only bites people who are where they've got no business being."

A few days later Dad got a letter from the woman inquiring about the health of the dog, for obvious reasons. Instead of simply assuring her that the dog was not rabid, he wrote her back saying, "Thank you for your concern about our dog. I am happy to tell you that it did not even make him sick."

So Dad's dealings with his "enemies" were sometimes less than Christ-like and instead, were more human, probably patterned somewhat after his family heritage. Dad once told me of his mother's uncle, Will Bennett, who, as the result of a disagreement with a neighbor, told the neighbor that if he ever set foot on his property again that he would kill him. He told the neighbor this knowing full well that the neighbor's closest route to the mailbox was across his property. So our dear old uncle watched the next day and, sure enough, there came the neighbor across the field on his way to get the mail.

The way old Uncle Will told the story was that he then loaded his flintlock rifle, steadied it on the front gate post, aimed it at the neighbor's head, cocked it, and pulled the trigger. Then he said, "I decided that I wasn't going to send my soul to hell for that no-good so-and-so, and I grabbed the hammer before the gun could fire." Quite a tall tale, undoubtedly, but it told volumes about Dad's gene pool.

Another story which is substantiated in local historic accounts tells of the unusual death of Dad's great grandfather, Jefferson Bennett. According to Dad, when he was a little boy, he was walking down the street in Hinton with his mother (Jane Bennett Dodd) when she pointed to an old man and said, "there is the man who killed your great granddaddy."

According to the family story, as told by my Grandmother to Dad, her Granddaddy Jeff was a leader of the Secessionists in Summers County when the Civil War broke out and he sent her father, Robert Bennett to fight for the Confederacy. Sam Richmond who lived in the New River valley and operated a mill at Richmond Falls (now called Sandstone Falls) was the leading Unionist and sent his son Tuck off to fight for the Union. After the war, Jeff was in his yard, washing his hands in preparation for supper, when a returning Union soldier shot him dead.

There may be even more to this story. It seems that, during the war, Sam Richmond had been mysteriously killed and the crime had never been solved and there was considerable speculation that his chief rival, Jeff Bennett just might have had something to do with it. The man that Grandma pointed out to Dad as the killer of her grandfather was Tuck Richmond, the Union soldier son of Sam Richmond.

Dad never shot anybody but his rifle standing beside the back door did come in handy once in awhile. After Momma's death, Dad lived alone at the old farm house for all but the last few months of his remaining eight years. During this time he continued as many of his normal activities as he could. Even when his health deteriorated to the point that he had to use a walker, he continued to raise a garden. He would use the walker to get to his tiller, and then, after somehow getting the motor started, he would hold on to the tiller and follow it as it jerked and thrashed through his rocky garden.

One year he was having a running feud with a groundhog that he was constantly complaining about, and every time I talked to him by phone he reiterated that "that pleg-ged (plagued) groundhog is eatin' up my garden."

On our next visit to see Dad, he proudly announced that he and his twenty-two caliber rifle had finished off the pesky groundhog that morning. "He stood up down at the far end of the garden and I must have hit him square between the eyes, for he dropped in his tracks and didn't even make it back to his hole," Dad crowed.

"Wow!" Rose said, "You must be a great shot."

"No," Dad responded, "I've been shooting at him all Summer. The law of averages finally got him."

Along about this same time in Dad's life, a group of con artists swept through Griffith Creek and Clayton preying on the defenseless older residents. They drove up to Dad's house and asked him if he would give them two dollars for the last remaining bit of paving material they had on their truck after finishing a job. Dad told them that, if they would smooth it out, he "reckoned" they could dump it behind the house where he parked his car. They had him sign a paper "giving permission" and then dumped a small amount of material, patted it down, and presented Dad with a bill for $200.

Dad could get indignant quickly, and he did.

"Look, old man," he was told as three large, menacing men closed in around him, "you signed a contract and if you don't pay, you will end up in jail. Either you give us the money or we are going to call the sheriff."

"Tell you what," Dad said as he reached inside the back door and brought out his groundhog shooting rifle, "I'll gonna go call him for you."

By the time he had the sheriff on the line, the "pavers" were out the driveway and on their way. The sheriff told Dad that he had just heard from some of Dad's neighbors who had been intimidated into paying the scammers. "It sounds like they tangled with the wrong person, though, when they tried to bluff you," the sheriff told Dad.

The tendency to hold grudges caused problems and pain in Dad's immediate family. Dad's brother, Reginald, who was eleven months older than Dad lived at Organ Cave, about twenty five miles from us, but I only saw him two or three times in my life.

The reason grew out of a family dispute at the time of my grandmother's death in 1940. Grandma, Jane Bennett Dodd, was terminally ill in the old Hinton Hospital and was constantly surrounded by three of her children, Dad, Aunt Gladys, and Uncle Larry, but not even visited by Uncle Reggie. This got Grandma so fired up at Reggie that she called in her lawyer to change her will and she divided most of her things three, rather than four, ways.

Uncle Reggie never got over it. For the most part, he just avoided the family. Dad and Momma made many attempts to restore good relations with him and his wife but were unsuccessful. When they would go to Reggie's house, they would be talked to briefly in the yard but never invited into his home. Although Reggie was a very intelligent and talented man, his life of resentment, along with his two most faithful companions, politics and alcohol, did not serve him well.

All this is background for a series of events which brought about a measure of reconciliation.

"Reginald's house burned this morning."
Momma's diary, January 26, 1958

"Dad and Paul went to see where Reginald's house burned down. Didn't get to see Reg or Hazel."
Momma's diary: January 27, 1958

When Dad and Reggie were about sixty, Dad got a heart-rending letter from Reggie's wife, Hazel. She said that now that their house had burned they had lost everything. Uncle Reggie was unemployed because his party had lost the governorship in the last election and his job had always been as a political appointee. He was broke and in failing health. Aunt Hazel concluded the letter by saying that Reggie's life would have been different "if you and your brother and sister had not cheated Reggie out of his inheritance."

The accusation about the "lost inheritance" would have been downright funny if it had not been so tragic. The entire estate was probably worth less than three thousand dollars, so what Uncle Reggie had lost for his inattention to his mother was a only a few hundred dollars.   But the tragedy was not the money, it was the hurt, the loneliness, the broken fellowship, the brooding, and, who knows, maybe even the drinking. Now this man who was once considered dashing and dapper was old before his time, sick, broke, childless, and homeless, with only two things in the world; his grudge against his family, and a wife who was apparently as bitter as he.

This came at a time when Momma and Dad were in the best financial condition of their lives.   About 1950, Dad began working more and more off the farm and by the time of Uncle Reggie's fire, they had saved a little bit of money. Dad was working as a bookkeeper for a construction firm so, after getting in touch with Reggie and assessing the situation, he and Momma did not hesitate, they used their savings to hire the firm that Dad worked for to immediately begin construction on a house for Reggie and Hazel.

"I haven't worked much today, just took it easy. Guess I must be lazy. We got a nice letter from Hazel."
Momma's diary: February 5, 1958

I did get one thing out of Uncle Reggie's feud with his mother, though. Since I slept with Momma and Dad most of the time for the first three years of my life, although I do not remember Grandma's passing, I do have a recollection of when her bed came into our house and the bed that Momma and Dad had in their bedroom was moved upstairs. It was not until I was grown that I realized that Grandma's bed was an antique brass bed. Both of my sisters let our parents know that they would someday like to own the bed and some of the granddaughters in the family also expressed some interest.

I was dumbfounded, then, to find in Dad's will that I was named, specifically. to receive the bed. It was the only item of furniture that was mentioned in his will. The mystery was solved a few days later as we were sorting through all of Momma's and Dad's papers to decide what to keep and what to put on the bonfire, when we found a letter to Dad from Reggie, dated in 1940. In the letter, Reggie thanked Dad for notifying him of the contents of their mother's will and acknowledged that the only item that he had been left was the brass bed. He further wrote that he did not want the bed and instructed Dad to "give it to Paul."

Suddenly, as I read that old letter, I had some new mysteries. Why would my uncle leave a bed to a two year old? Was this an expression of his feelings for me? Was I the only person in the family that he felt was less deserving than he? Was this an act of contempt, or love, or something else? And why didn't Dad or Momma ever tell anyone, especially me, the story of the bed?

Dad was very political and it is hard to be political and not have enemies. He often was chosen to work on election days at the one room school which was the polling place in our community. This crimped Dad's style since he had to sit in the school house counting votes instead of being out "hauling voters" to the polls who would vote for the Democrats. And this was doubly bitter because his great friend/enemy, Arnold Harris, was breaking every speed limit dashing up and down the road hauling in loads of Republicans.

Dad was a lifelong Democrat. His heroes ranged from William Jennings Bryan to Harry Truman. William Jennings Bryan held a special place in Dad's heart, since when he was the Democratic presidential nominee for the third time in 1908, Dad was 9 years old and politically aware for the first time.

A few years later, Dad experienced a great moment when, as a teenager, he got to see the eminent Mr. Bryan and hear him give a command performance of his famous "Cross of Gold" speech as part of a touring Chautauqua group which came and set up its large tent to bring culture to West Virginia.

Momma, who was raised in a Republican family faithfully became a Democrat after her marriage as well as being baptized by immersion and becoming a Baptist. So Momma was officially a Democrat and a Baptist, but maybe not enough of either one to be nasty. As a matter of fact, I think that she held some of the teachings of the Methodists as long as she lived, and occasionally was pleased when the Republicans did well.

As far as I know, Dad voted for one Republican in his life. One year, as usual, he had worked at the polls for a primary election and then had the task of delivering the ballots to the Summers County Court House. Arriving there about midnight, he was immediately called to by one of the Democratic candidates for County Assessor. "Hey, Dodd, how did I do up at Griffith Creek?" he asked. "Well sir," Dad told him, "there were exactly one hundred votes cast and you got one of them."

"That's about what I expected from you and that bunch of ignorant (censored, censored, censored, censored) riff-raff that lives up there," the candidate raged.

Much to Dad's chagrin, that man got the Democratic nomination for County Assessor. So, Dad voted for a Republican. And he did not stop there. At that time he had a job which took him all over the county and he told and retold that story countless times to anyone who would listen and when the votes for the general election were counted, thanks to Dad's campaigning, Summers County had a Republican Assessor.

"We got up at 4:30. Dad got off to the election in good time. I churned and fixed his dinner. Shelby took me to vote and take his dinner to him. I came home and did my ironing. Brought up the cows, milked and have the work done up. Arthur got home after 9 o'clock. **The Republicans are ahead.**

Momma's diary: November 4, 1958

Momma's goodness won out over Dad's inherent tendencies in most cases, but occasionally there was a situation that even Momma's prayers and pleading could not fully resolve.

It was about 1942 that Dad entered into a verbal, gentlemen's agreement with a neighbor named Will Stevens to farm a sixty acre abandoned orchard that adjoined our farm. No money changed hands since the agreement was that Mr. Stevens would be paid proportionately out of any profit made from the land. They further agreed that, after the deed to the property was cleared by settling the Stevens family estate, Dad could buy the property. The parcel was a nearly level plateau on top of the mountain above our home. Compared to eking out a living on our small, stony, steep fields, Dad knew that farming "the orchard" would be like paradise.

The first job was to clear the sixty acres and get it ready to farm. There were old diseased fruit trees to cut and burn. There were hardwood saplings as large as four inches in diameter that Dad had to dig around with a mattock, chop the roots with an axe, and then pull with John and Nell, his team of gray horses. Dad worked all winter from daylight to dark clearing and "grubbing" the orchard property. My oldest brother, Junior, was away at college so James was Dad's main help. As soon as James got off the school bus each day he would run up the hill to help Dad and they worked together there every Saturday.

By the time for Spring planting, there were gigantic piles of old trees and brush to burn in preparation for plowing. About twenty acres, or one third of the land had been cleared and was plowed, harrowed, and planted primarily to field corn and sorghum cane, with a few small plots of other crops that first year. The crops were harvested by hand and hauled off the mountain by our horse drawn wagon. The sorghum was brought to the cane mill and furnace behind our house where it was crushed for its sweet juice and boiled into molasses. The profits from all crops were dutifully shared with Mr. Stevens.

That fall, the first twenty acres were seeded to wheat and interseeded with clover and timothy. The clover and timothy would grow into a perennial hay crop after the wheat was harvested early the next summer. That winter was spent getting the next twenty acres ready for spring planting. More cutting, digging, pulling, piling, and burning but the reward was another bumper crop of corn and sorghum to go with the bounty of twenty acres of wheat. Work went a lot slower, though, for this was the summer that Dad lost his helper when James was drafted into the Navy and Dad began breaking in his daughters, Leora and Rhodetta, as his new farm hands.

By the end of the third winter, the entire sixty acres were cleared and ready for full production. The first twenty acres were growing clover and timothy hay, the second twenty acres were in wheat, and the last twenty acres were planted to corn and sorghum.

On a bright day in late May, Dad hitched the horses to the mowing machine, drove them up the steep farm road to the "orchard" and started mowing hay. I was almost six years old and was honored that Dad let me go with him. The hay crop was tremendous. It was so heavy in places that he had to slap the horses with the ends of the check lines to make them trot in order to get the cutter blade moving fast enough to cut through the growth. Each time he would make a round and come near to where I was playing, he would yell out "Yip-pee." He was in his glory.

We had not been there very long that morning until we had a visitor. Mr. Stevens, himself, came by to pay us a visit. As soon as Dad saw him he stopped the horses, got off the mowing machine and greeted him with a big smile. All I remember about the events that followed is that Dad suddenly got very angry, became very loud, and shouted that he was going to "mow that hay, anyway, and you can't stop me," but after a long argument, he raised the cutter bar on the mower, headed the horses down the hill toward home and said to me in an emotional voice, "Let's go." I asked, "Why?" and he just repeated, "Let's go."

When we got home Dad was still boiling. He told Momma that Mr. Stevens had ordered him off the property and told him that he would not be permitted to harvest the crops which were growing and would never be permitted to farm the land again. When Dad had asked him why he was doing this Mr. Stevens said that he did not think that he had received his fair share from the sorghum crop last year.

That accusation should have insulted Momma as much as it did Dad since she was a full partner in the molasses making and was the one who did the canning and bottling of it and kept count of the amount. But instead of being insulted, she immediately started to decide the best way to offer the other cheek, but Dad would have none of it. I think that he was, mentally, loading the rifle and steadying it on the gate post. He wanted satisfaction.

When we sat down to our noon meal, Dad was still ranting. Momma finally asked him, "You wouldn't really want to do anything to hurt Mr. Stevens, would you?"

"I'd rather lick him than eat," Dad bellowed, as he stomped away from the table.

The "orchard" saga was a bitter pill for Dad to swallow. Now, just across the fence from our little three acre "pear tree" field, we could only watch as the clover and timothy matured and fell over, we watched as the wheat went unharvested, we watched the weeds choke out the corn and sorghum, and then watched for years as the entire area grew up, once again, into a thicket of trees and brush.

Dad handled it in his own way. He never shot anybody, nor did he "lick" anybody, despite how much he had wanted to. What he did was to shun Mr. Stevens. He never spoke of him and, on the few occasions in which I saw them in the same vicinity, Dad never spoke to him. Dad simply ignored him. Momma tried many times to change Dad's behavior, but with no results.

Some years later, we were in the middle of a revival meeting at our church and no one was getting saved. The evangelist somehow concluded that the fact that no one was getting saved could not possibly be related to his preaching, so it must be because someone in the church was "harboring sin." He repeated this night after unproductive night until one of the church members went to the evangelist and told him that the only thing he could think of was that Arthur Dodd was not on speaking terms with Will Stevens.

"Aha," said the evangelist, triumphantly, "that's it!" Brother Dodd was the stumbling block. So Dad was confronted by the evangelist about his treatment of his "brother," Will Stevens.

Dad got dressed for church a little early the next evening and, saying that he would be back in a few minutes, drove off in the opposite direction from the church. When he returned, there, sitting in the front seat of the old Chevy beside Dad, was Will Stevens. Dad took him to church, sat with him, and took him home. That was the only time in my life that I ever saw Mr. Stevens in a church service other than at a funeral. I would love to have heard the conversation between Dad and Mr. Stevens that caused him to go to church that night. It is just possible that Dad gave him the choice of going to church or "taking a licking." Dad could hold a grudge.

Momma was never satisfied with Dad's treatment of Mr. Stevens. When she pressed the issue with him, Dad said, "I don't hate the man, but I do hate what he did to me. When a man treats a person the way he treated me, the best thing you can do is to just leave him alone."

Dad was tough, and stubborn in a righteous way, but Momma was different. Although the accusation was potentially as insulting to her as it was to Dad, she never missed an opportunity to speak to Mr. Stevens and would go out of her way to visit with him, inquire about his health, and wish him well.

I also never heard her say anything bad about him, nor anyone else, and she gently, but consistently, urged Dad to do likewise.

Like Momma said, *"As far as I know, I don't have an enemy in the world. I have searched my heart and I am sure of one thing; I love everybody."*

6 THOU SHALT NOT SMOKE OR CHEW, AND DRINKING IS OUT OF THE QUESTION

"Whether therefore ye eat, or drink, or whatsoever ye do, do all to the glory of God." I Corinthians 10:31
Scripture often quoted by Momma

Dad loved Florida. Sometime around 1910, when Dad was ten or eleven, his Uncle John had given up trying to make a living on his mountain farm at Jumping Branch and had relocated his family to Seminole County, in central Florida. Uncle John had a large family and any contact that Dad had with them through the years just whetted his appetite to see the wonders of what sounded like paradise. When his Uncle John would come back to West Virginia for a visit, Dad would marvel at his descriptions of level land, palm trees, orange groves, warm winters, and the biggest fish he had ever heard of.

Once, when Dad was a teenager, his cousin Berman stopped in West Virginia on his way to New York City for a "prize fight." Dad often told us how Berman removed his shirt so Dad's family could admire how the muscles on his back rippled when he flexed. Berman continued to box until the fateful day that he got into the ring with the great Jack Johnson and decided that, if he ever recovered, he would give up the sport and become a beekeeper.

Going to Florida to see it for himself was a long time dream for Dad, but just did not seem possible until the late 1940's when, for the first time, Dad had a little bit of money and a car that could be trusted to go farther than from Griffith Creek to Hinton. He really got the bug after we were visited by his cousin Corbett who told us about the three dairy farms that he and his brother and brother-in-law had around a large lake, and about his cattle ranch, his orange trees, his pineapple patch, and especially about the livestock market that he had just built which could use Dad's expertise as a manager.

"Let's go to Florida," he said to Momma, for the first time, in 1948.

"I don't think that I want to go that far away from home," was her response, "but why don't you go on and Paul and I will take care of things here."

Not wanting to go alone, Dad invited his good friends Clint and Mamie Harvey to accompany him as he went to the land of his dreams for a ten day visit. It was even greater than he had imagined. He was able to see for himself the ocean, wild alligators, majestic Brahma cattle, and, miracle of miracles, flat-land farming. He brought back pictures of the Bok Singing Tower, hoop-skirted models at Cypress Gardens, and glass-bottomed boats at Silver Springs. He ate oranges and grapefruit that he picked from the trees, sliced pineapples from Corbett's garden, and discovered the greatest of all "comfort foods," grits. All of his Florida relatives were prosperous and treated him like a king. And he couldn't wait to take Momma there so he could experience it with her.

But she resisted. So the next year he went without her. And the next, and the next and the next. At last, in the winter of 1954, after six years of urging, Momma agreed to embark on the great adventure and accompany Dad on a visit to his Garden of Eden, Florida.

They had only traveled sixty miles from home when their car was crowded by another driver and Dad lost control and they plummeted into a deep road ditch. I was called out of first period class at high school, picked up by brother Arthur Jr., and we subsequently picked up James, Leora, and Rhodetta, and Junior drove as fast as the crooked roads would permit until we arrived at the hospital in Covington, Virginia.

We got to Momma's room first and, in her typical fashion, she gave us an optimistic report. She informed us that the extent of her injuries was a compound fracture of her left ankle and two broken teeth. She said that the ankle did not hurt much now, and smiled when she told us the broken teeth did not hurt at all since, of course, they were dentures. The doctor had told her that Dad had been injured by slamming into the steering wheel when the car hit the bottom of the ravine and he had broken his breast bone, collar bone, and a number of ribs, but that his life was not in danger. So we left Momma's room cheered and greatly relieved.

But when we got to Dad's room, it was a different story. Dad had always been the world's loudest sufferer, but due to the limits on his lung capacity by the broken ribs, it was not loud, but it was the most pitiful moaning and groaning you ever heard. "I'm glad you kids got here when you did," he wailed, "for I'm a goner this time."

"But, Dad," I said, "the doctors say that you are going to be all right."

"They don't know nothing, boy. I'm telling you, this is it. I'm done for." was his plaintive reply.

So there he lay in terrible pain, moaning and groaning, breathing as lightly as possible because every time he breathed the ends of his broken ribs clicked audibly against each other, convinced that he was at death's door, when a Virginia State Policeman came into his room to investigate the accident.

"Tell me, Dodd," the officer brusquely asked, "when did you have your last drink?"

In spite of pain, drugs, and feeling certain that his next breath might be his last, Dad did not hesitate. "June 30, 1918," was his immediate reply. The officer who had began his inquiry so sternly, showed a slight smile and remarked that "it doesn't appear that alcohol was a factor," and proceeded with another line of questioning.

The rest of that story was that Dad and Momma were married on July 10, 1918, just ten days after that last drink that was so precisely remembered. Momma had made her acceptance of Dad's proposal of marriage conditional; she would marry him only if he would stop drinking. It worked. In fact, it worked so well that she once told me that she wished that she had included smoking in the bargain. "But," she said, "I was sure that he loved me so much that after we were married, all I would have to say was, 'Honey, why don't you quit smoking,' and he would quit."

However, it did not work out as easily had Momma had it planned. She did ask him and ask him and ask him, and he did quit, but it took thirty-five years. I would never accuse Momma of being a nag on the subject, but she certainly was persistent.

65

Dad did not get to show Momma the wonders of Florida that year, but two years later they did share a memorable trip there together, the highlight of which, according to Momma, was seeing the ocean for the very first time and then, kicking off her shoes and holding Dad's hand, wading in the foamy surf at Cocoa Beach.

Momma's beliefs about the evils of tobacco and alcohol were not grounded in the extensive medical reports that form the basis of today's rationale for avoiding them. She did not need a medical report. Her beliefs began with two scripture passages that she often cited on the subject: I Corinthians 6:19 and 20: "Know ye not that your body is the temple of the Holy Spirit which is in you, which ye have of God and ye are not your own? For ye are bought with a price: therefore glorify God in your body," and I Corinthians 10:31: "Whether therefore ye eat, or drink, or whatsoever ye do, do all for the glory of God."

She could not see how engaging in activities solely for the purpose of satisfying self and activities which she believed to be harmful to the body could be done to the glory of God. Therefore, to Momma, both activities were sinful.

She was way ahead of her time on health and addiction. Her belief that smoking was related to health problems was largely ignored, and even ridiculed at times. Our neighbor, Arnold Harris, was a leader in our church and he loved to sing. He had a beautiful tenor voice and prided himself on hitting the high harmony part of the old songs we sang in church. I remember hearing him and Dad singing in a male quartet with Elmer Graham and Buz Rogers and I thought they would raise the roof right off the church. Arnold, like Dad, was a smoker.

Each year at Christmas, Dad gave small gifts to members of his adult Sunday School class. Since Arnold was a special friend and also our mailman, Dad's gift to him was always larger and was often a carton or two of cigarettes. Yes, cigarettes, in their special Christmas packages with big red ribbons on them, given openly and proudly right there in church and nobody seemed to think that there was anything inappropriate about it, except Momma. After all, the preacher smoked, Dad smoked, Arnold smoked, and virtually every other man in the church smoked.

The fifteen minute intermission between Sunday School and "preaching" was used by the men of the church, the pastor included, to gather under the big oak trees and smoke before going into the worship service. When I was small, we never had a pastor who demanded a salary. It was generally believed, at that time and place, that a salary for the pastor was unscriptural and, instead of a salary, he was given a love offering collected during the intermission and Dad had the task of collecting it. I remember him going from man to man as they stood smoking and talking under the oak trees, collecting a dollar or two from each and recording the contributions in his little Royster fertilizer book. I can still see him as he carried out this sacred duty; dressed in his dark blue suit with a white shirt and tie, and always with a cigarette hanging from the corner of his mouth.

As time passed, Arnold's beautiful tenor voice became raspy and he started to have chronic throat problems. Not only would he sometimes not sing, often he would not talk. Momma operated on the theory that just maybe there was a connection between Arnold's throat problems and his heavy smoking. When she advanced her theory to Dad, he dismissed it without any discussion. I even tried to reason with her. "Smoking doesn't hurt anybody," I confidently postulated, "it doesn't do a person any good, but it doesn't hurt them. Everybody smokes!"

But that did not stop Momma. She confronted Arnold with her theory at church one night and encouraged him to think about quitting smoking. Arnold was gentle with her, maybe even condescending, as he smiled and explained to her in a voice that was barely audible that his only problem was that when he sang he strained his voice. He said that his doctor had told him to stop singing but certainly had not told him to stop smoking for, after all, the doctor smoked, too.

Some years later, when Dad finally came to the realization that smoking was damaging his health and he heeded Momma's persistent advice to quit smoking, the first person he went to was Arnold. Like all zealous new converts, Dad could not wait to share with his friend the joys of his new found freedom from the smoking habit and the resultant rediscovery of his taste buds. But, alas, it did no good. Dad was crushed. He said that he was sure that if he could quit smoking, he could convince anyone else to quit, too.

Dad lived twenty-eight years after he quit smoking, yet his death was due to a hemorrhage of his lungs caused by lung cancer. Only recently have medical studies shown that smoking may, in some people, create circumstances which will result in cancer many years after a person stops smoking. Momma knew something that the doctors and medical researchers did not know and she knew it long before they discovered it in the early 1960's: smoking is bad for your health and it may even kill you.

Momma understood addictive personality, too. Her advice regarding both tobacco and alcohol was to "never start." She realized that there were people who drank alcohol moderately, but she also knew a number of people whose lives and families had been destroyed because they had "formed the habit" and could not control their need for alcohol. She did not despise or reject those who were addicted to alcohol, instead she showed compassion to them. But she believed firmly that they were controlled by the alcohol and the only way they would ever be delivered from their addiction was by God's direct intervention.

With this insight into Momma's beliefs regarding the hazards connected to smoking and drinking, and her commitment to the messages in I Corinthians, it should not come as any surprise that her instruction to her children, her Sunday School Class, and anyone else who would listen was always very precise and to the point.

"Don't ever start," she continually advised. "You don't know how it will affect you and if it gets hold of you and you 'form the habit' you may never be able to stop and it could destroy your life."

Her other advice was based on her practical application of the passages from I Corinthians. "When you are tempted to try something that you think may be wrong, before you try it, stop and give thanks to God for it. If you cannot give thanks for it, you should leave it alone," she would advise.

Despite the fact that Dad smoked until after my brothers and sisters were grown and away from home and I was a teenager, none of us ever became smokers. My two brothers saw active duty in World War II and neither returned home a smoker or drinker. They used the cigarettes which were given to them by the tobacco companies as a means of barter.

Junior traded a carton of cigarettes for an album of 78 rpm records of Christmas songs performed by Bing Crosby and the Andrews Sisters which we played each Christmas for years on our old wind-up Victrola. These were the same great renditions of "White Christmas," "Adeste Fideles," "Jingle Bells," "Santa Claus is Coming to Town," and others, which are now sold on tapes and CD's. James brought back a guitar from Italy, the purchase price of which had also been a carton of cigarettes.

So none of us took up drinking or smoking, but it was probably not Momma's "foreknowledge" about health and addictive personality that kept us from it. I believe that the biggest reason was that we did not want to disappoint her. I also believe that she hammered enough of her theology based on I Corinthians into us that we could never be comfortable doing it.

I think that maybe that guy Sigmund Freud was on to something: our conscience often is the voice of our Mother.

7 TRAIN UP A CHILD IN THE WAY HE SHOULD GO, AND "NO, YOU ARE NOT MY FAVORITE"

"So thankful for each of our dear loved ones. Our sweet children are so thoughtful of Dad and myself. May God bless each of them and their families.

Momma's writings: Christmas 1962

An elderly woman once asked Dad if he believed the Bible. "I sure do," was his prompt reply. "Do you believe all of it?" she continued. "Yes, ma'am," he said, confidently, "I believe every word of it! I believe it from cover to cover!"

"Do you believe Proverbs 22:6?" she asked. "That's where it says to 'train up a child in the way he should go: and when he is old, he will not depart from it.'"

"Yes, ma'am, I do," Dad said.

"Then, explain my son to me," she said. "I raised him in the church, I told him about Jesus, and I have prayed for him every day of his life. Yet, he has lived an awful life. He has been mean to me, he left his wife and children years ago, and now he is in prison. I raised him right but it didn't make any difference. Why didn't God do what he said he would do? I just don't know what to believe anymore,"

Dad did not get stumped very often, but he was stumped that time. He gave the woman some standard platitudes about not giving up and her son's life not being over yet, but he was stumped and he knew it. "I wasn't going to tell her that God failed, because God never fails," he said later. "But I couldn't tell the woman that she had failed, either, because I didn't know how she had raised her son."

That episode has caused me to think a lot about that scripture passage over the years and I have observed many instances where it worked just like the woman thought it should, but I have also seen where it did not seem to work. Sometimes within a single family, one child is true to the faith of the parents and another goes away from the faith and dies out there. Is each of the thousands of proverbs in the book of Proverbs a sacred iron-clad covenant promise from God or are they inspired generalities written by Solomon the wise man which are excellent guides to life, and, if followed, will usually produce the desired result?

I am not going to answer that for you, but let me assure you that Momma saw that proverb about "training up a child" as a contract between her and God. She took the task of "mothering" very seriously.

Momma identified strongly with Hannah, the mother of Samuel, in the Old Testament. Because of the difficulties they experienced during the first five years of their marriage, she and Dad feared that they would never have any children. So, when we finally came along, boy, were we special. I guess that I grew up assuming that all children was made to feel special just the way we were. What I did not know until I was old enough to begin to look at the world realistically was that what was really special was the way in which Momma raised us.

As I was searching through the various things which Momma left behind, I found "Ten Commandments for Parents," in her handwriting, folded in an one of her old Bibles. Momma wore out a lot of Bibles and after they became tattered and torn, instead of disposing of them, she just put them on a shelf, where they remained until now just to provide me with priceless "time capsules" containing her miscellaneous writings. The first page of this Bible was inscribed, "presented to Bertha Dodd as a wedding anniversary gift," in handwriting that was not Momma's. Just under that inscription, in Momma's handwriting was, "by Ruby Lacy."

As I have reconstructed the events which led to this gift, Momma must have been Ruby's secret "Circle Sister" for the year in which the Bible was given. At the end of the year when the "secret" was revealed, Momma had written in the name of the giver. Ruby Lacy moved from our community when I was seven years old when her husband, Marvin, gave up his education career as the teacher at the one room Griffith Creek Grade School to begin his political career in the position of

Office Deputy to Summers County Sheriff, Earl Hellems.

The gift of this Bible must date to the early or mid-1940's, so if the writing dates back to the time of the gift, Momma raised me with this information in mind. I do not think the following is original with Momma and I have no idea of its source, but believe me, it is vintage Momma. (The parenthetical comments are mine.)

Ten Commandments for Parents

1. Thou shalt look upon thy child, not as a possession belonging to thee, but as a sacred trust from God. (She did!)

2. Thou shalt be honest in all dealings with thy children, then honesty and obedience can be expected of them. (She was!)

3. Thou shalt regard thy child's respect and love, not as duty to be demanded, but as an achievement to be earned. (She earned it!)

4. Remember when you are out of patience with thy child's faults to take time to count ten . . . . of thine own. (This was one of her favorites)

5. Remember that the surest way to make it hard for thy child is to make it too easy. The child should learn early the meaning of discipline and responsibility. (She must have had this one memorized; she never made it easy)

6. Thou shalt have daily prayer and Bible reading with the family and thou shalt always thank God for food before partaking of it. (She never failed)

7. Thou shalt early teach thy child to love and trust in God, and thou shalt wisely help thy child to choose Jesus Christ as Savior and Lord. (She taught)

8. Remember that the example of thy life is more effective than thy fault finding and moralizing. (She set quite an example!)

9. Thou shalt practice the teachings of Jesus in thy home be being kind, unselfish, and loving. (She exhibited these, and all other fruits of the Spirit)

10. Remember the Sabbath Day by worshipping God in thy church as a family, for this is necessary if thy home is to be truly Christian. (We did)

Undated. Folded sheet in old Bible

Looking back, I know that she followed those "Ten

Commandments" very closely. They also provide the perfect background for some specific principles which I observed her following, consistently and constantly, as she "brought us up," and that I would like to discuss more fully.

Principle No. 1. Love your children, and let them know that you love them.

Since I was the last child by quite a few years, I had Momma all to myself most of the time. I was so confident of my position that, when I was about four or five years old, I asked Momma if I was her favorite child, very sure of a favorable response.

But Momma surprised me. She told me that she loved me very much and she tried to love all of her children "the same." "But," she added, "there is something special to a mother about her first child."

Her first child? Her first child? My brother that I hardly knew? My brother who left for college when I was two years old? The one who had driven the Model A Ford into the creek after he was told not to try to drive it? The one whose teenage conflicts with our parents were family legends? The most headstrong, opinionated member of the family? That first child?

The last couple of years of Momma's life were very revealing about her special feelings toward her first child. Her first-born, Arthur Jr., was killed in an auto accident, along with his son, Richard, exactly two years before Momma's death. At the time of this tragedy, Momma was suffering from an advanced case of Parkinson's Disease. We took her to the funeral services in a wheel chair and we could not tell just how much of the events she was capable of comprehending. Her conscious mind, though, was sharply focused on a two year period of her life, 1923 and 1924, the time of Junior's birth and infancy.

She had her old boxes of "things" brought to her and she searched until she found some small, oval framed pictures of her strikingly beautiful, bright-eyed, dark haired first child and had them placed on the coffee table where she could see them. And, although she would not know what day it was nor could she recall the name of the friend or family member she was talking to, she could give details of those days fifty years before as if they had just happened.

"He is the most beautiful baby there ever was." she would rhapsodize. "Everybody who sees him says so."

"I dress him up so cute and when it is time for his daddy to come home from work, we go to meet him. One day when Junior saw his daddy coming up the hill, he ran to meet him and fell and skinned his little knees. I hated that so bad."

"He is such a good little boy. Sometimes we take him to church twice on Sunday. Sometimes we go the Methodist Church in the morning and then to the Dunkard Church in the afternoon. He just sits there and listens. Everybody says that he is such a little man."

1923 and 1924 were the years that Dad and Momma lived in the little mountain community of Durbin, in Pocahontas County, West Virginia. Dad was a bookkeeper at the tannery. I was raised on stories of their lives there, so once when I was driving to college I decided to veer off from my usual route to Morgantown just to see the community. I found the tannery, the railroad station and the churches, all the landmarks of which I had heard. With that much information, Dad and Momma were able to tell me how to locate the little white house where they had lived, and on my next trip, I found it.

So, now, years later, as Momma was describing places and events about her life in Durbin, I could visualize them, but my sisters who had never been there could not. Just a couple of years ago, we spent one of the most memorable days of our lives. My two sisters and my brother-in-law Ralph, piled into the van with Rose and me and we went to Durbin. We went to the little house where they had lived. Although the current residents were not at home, we stood on the porch, walked around the house, and took lots of pictures. Standing there, we could see the nearby Methodist Church and the "Dunkard" (Church of the Brethren) Church at the top of the hill at the end of the street.

We walked down the hill toward the train station on the same street where our oldest brother had skinned his knees hurrying to meet his daddy. We could see the tannery down the river about two miles away and it was not hard to imagine seeing Dad walking home in his familiar gait and flashing his beautiful smile as he saw his young wife and little boy rushing to meet him.

Okay. So Junior was number one, and I had to admit that he was a wonder. Despite coming of age in the depths of the Great Depression, he earned the money and, against the wishes of his parents, managed to go to the World's Fair while in high school. As a teenager he somehow obtained a good quality camera and taught himself photography, all the way from composition to developing, to enlarging, to color tinting.

He was able to accomplish great things despite the fact that he was plagued by a terrible case of a Dodd family malady that was called "Sunday sick headaches," or "Grandma's blind spells," only he did not just have them on Sundays, he often had two or three a week. It was not until he was in the Navy that he got a more scientific diagnosis of the problem which was migraine headaches.

He was determined to go to college and he accomplished this by hitchhiking the two hundred miles back and forth between home and college, first at Potomac State College in Keyser and then at West Virginia University at Morgantown. He developed a hitchhiking technique during his freshman year which included dressing nicely, wearing his little gold and blue beanie, and prominently displaying his college insignia on his suitcase.

He mailed his dirty laundry home each week in a simulated leather laundry case. Momma would wash and iron his clothes, carefully fold them and place them in the case, reverse the little address card in the plastic window, and then, before closing the case and securing the straps around it, she would put in a small tin of love, containing cookies or homemade candy or fruitcake or whatever was fresh and shippable.

While at the university he worked as a waiter at Woman's Hall in return for his meals. He earned expense money by getting up at four o'clock in the morning and walking the four miles to the University dairy barns, working for two hours and then walking and running back to campus in time to clean up and go to class. All of that effort earned him a hefty twenty cents a day; he was paid ten cents an hour.

Junior was always building something. As a vocational agriculture project while he was in high school, he had planned and built, all by himself, a brooder house large enough to raise one hundred baby chickens. When he was in his late twenties he cut the trees from our farm, skidded the logs with Dad's horses, and had the logs sawed into lumber and then built his own house on a beautiful lot beside the Greenbrier River at Lowell that his father-in-law gave to him and Charlotte, his wife.

Twenty years later, after he and his family had moved to Jackson, Michigan, where he took a teaching position, Rose and the boys and I went to visit them and found him working on the house he had just bought. The house was newly built but not completely finished, so he was in his element. Within a couple of years, he decided that the house needed to be bigger, so he doubled the size of it. By the next year he was certain that the roof lines did not suit the house so he took off the entire top of the house and rebuilt it in one summer.

His neighbors told him he was crazy. What was he going to do when it rained? He told them it was a "work of faith" and he just kept working and the sun just kept shining and it did not rain until he had his beautiful, appropriate new roof on his house. I told him that when he got to Heaven and was given his mansion, his first reaction would be, "Where are the building supplies? This place needs some work."

He turned his hobby of photography into a profession and operated a photography business in Hinton for a number of years. He established an auto salvage business at Pence Springs, and, in a moment of political impulse, was almost elected to the West Virginia House of Delegates. At the time of his death he was a school principal in Michigan and had earned enough post graduate credits for a doctorate degree in education. Throughout his life he worked, schemed, and clawed in order to achieve his dreams against heavy odds, often including a lack of support or understanding from his parents. A combination of Momma's determination and Dad's stubbornness, he was a dynamo.

He was also, like Momma, a very outgoing, demonstrative person who readily shared his emotions and loved the attention of others. Whenever he came to see Momma, they always greeted each other with hugs and kisses and then repeated the process when he had to leave.

But if he was Momma's favorite, where did that leave the rest of us? Believe me, none of us ever suffered from a lack of love from Momma. She had plenty to go around, more than enough really, for it spilled over to include everyone she knew. Remember, she did not have any enemies.

"Arthur Jr., Charlotte, Sandra, and A. C. came and brought us a box of fruits from Fla. Showed pictures he had taken in Fla. and at Christmas. They are all so sweet."

Momma's diary: January 17, 1958

Principle No. 2: Recognize the uniqueness of each child and treat that child accordingly.

Like Momma said, she loved us all and somehow, she was able to treat us each in accordance with our varying personalities.

James, her second child, was the strong, silent type, a gentle giant, very different from the rest of us huggy-kissy extroverts. As a youngster he was too shy to eat at a friend's house. Even as a teenager he would not stay overnight away from home. Other than an unpleasant camping trip or two into the mountains with his adventurous older brother, he never spent a night away from home until he was drafted into the Navy.

He had a quiet, sly sense of humor which would sneak up on us when we least expected it. He and Junior had a lot of disagreements as boys and some pretty serious fights, often due to James' chicanery. When they were in their early teens, they agreed to cut each other's hair and James got to do the first cutting. After surveying the job he had done on his older brother, he decided that he did not need a haircut after all and took off into the woods.

I think that the last fight they had was when Junior was in college and deeply in love with a girl named Betty. All he could talk about was "Betty." So when Junior came home and found that James had, for some unknown reason, named his Vo-Ag project brood sow "Betty," he was bent on getting satisfaction.

James graduated from Talcott High school in May, 1943, just one week before his eighteenth birthday on June 1. On the morning of his birthday, as he and Dad were getting ready to drive to Hinton for James to register for the draft, James asked Dad if he could drive. Slowly the old Model-A Ford crept down the road as James drove for the very first time. This was in sharp contrast to his older brother who had driven the same car into the creek before his sixteenth birthday.

At the end of World War II, after nearly three years of homesickness and seasickness, James returned home. I know that he was seasick because after making three round trips across the Atlantic Ocean as a gunner, he was asked by an uncle if he ever got seasick. "Yes," he replied. "Three times over and three times back."

I know that he was homesick too, because once he got home, he never wanted to leave again. When he was discharged, Dad asked him what he wanted to do and encouraged him to take advantage of the G. I.

Bill and go to college. "No," he said, "all I want to do is live here and farm. I am going to live just like I never left." And that is precisely what he did.

What had been "Grandma's place," which had been paid for largely by James' allotment checks, now became "James' place." He worked weekends and nights for months modernizing the old house. He jacked up the sagging floor joists, redid the electrical wiring, put in insulation, put sheet-rock on the walls and ceilings, installed a bathroom and modern kitchen, and painted, sanded, and roofed until the old place was beautiful. So beautiful, in fact, he and his bride, Mary Elizabeth, spent their honeymoon there.

The only other move he made in his life was to the adjoining larger farm which he bought from Noah Flint when Mr. Flint's health began to fail. This farm, more than two hundred acres located on a picturesque mountain top plateau, was made for James and he was made for it.

He built a pond for a water supply for his livestock and as a place for his family to fish and swim. He built diversion terraces and farmed the big fields in long, graceful contour strips across the slope to control erosion. As a result of his work, he was selected as the outstanding Conservation Farmer for Summers County for a number of years. He built up to a herd of sixty to eighty cattle, mostly purebred Herefords, and a flock of about one hundred and fifty sheep.

It seemed as if, to those around James, the war years had never occurred. After his death, I was talking with Linda, his oldest daughter, and I asked her how much her dad had told her of his war time experiences. Specifically, I wanted to know if he had told her about the ships being torpedoed around him, or his visit to Mt. Vesuvius, or his experiences in Africa, or especially his trip to Jerusalem where he had been able to crawl into the sepulcher where it is believed that Jesus was buried.

"No," she said, very surprised, "he never, ever mentioned any of those things." These were things he had talked about when he came home on leave, but once the war was over, they evidently were stored deep in his brain, never again to be retrieved.

Momma was convinced that James' wartime service led to his health problems and early death. When he returned from his second trans-Atlantic tour of duty, something very strange happened; his hair died. I mean that it dried up, crinkled, broke off, and fell out, in that order. Baldness was not a family trait so this occurrence was a mystery.

When he was diagnosed with cancer when he was forty-four years old, he was initially told that he had sarcoma, or bone cancer. Before he died, a mere six months later, he had symptoms of myaloma and possibly other forms of the disease. Once when Dad and I talked to his doctor about his condition, the doctor was clearly excited about his case and went on and on about his unique symptoms, the experimental treatments, and various test results which were producing some of the highest readings ever recorded. He was so enthusiastic that Dad asked, "Do you mean that he might whip this thing?"

"Oh, no," the doctor replied, "he can't survive this, but we have never seen anything like his case before."

Momma's theory, and I agree with her, was that James was exposed to something on his second trans-Atlantic tour that not only killed his hair, but in the long run killed him, too. My guess is that the ship on which he was assigned was carrying radioactive materials, the dangers of which were unknown at the time.

Momma and James had a special relationship. She respected his unique personality and treated him as if she could read his mind. While the rest of us got lots of warm hugs and kisses from Momma, she had to be content to show her affection to James with a pat on the arm or shoulder. She and the rest of her children could have very personal conversations about emotions and feelings and even about religious experiences, but she did not have this type of conversation with him. Instead, she showed her love to him by being sensitive to his needs, which although unspoken were clearly understood by her.

They communicated through their shared joy in work and accomplishment. He inherited her enthusiasm for work and, like her, had an uncanny ability to do at least twice as much work as anyone else. When I came along, all slow-pokey and day-dreamy, I was constantly reminded of how quickly and efficiently James would have done my assigned work when he was my age.

Momma and James also communicated through food; she would cook it and he would devour it. Long after he had married and moved into his own home, Momma said that she still missed him going to the garden and bringing in an arm load of greens, or squash, or parsnips, or whatever struck his fancy and telling her exactly how he wanted her to prepare it for him for supper.

Momma did not let World War II completely break down her communication through food that she had going with both of her older sons. She knew that it was not possible to send them all of the traditional Christmas goodies that they loved, but she knew that canned goods could be sent to them. So she made up a batch of her personal best fruit cake batter, took it to the cannery in Alderson where it was canned and baked and then she mailed Christmas fruit cakes as love packages to her boys. They both told her that they made many friends by sharing pieces of their delicious, cylindrical fruit cakes with their fellow sailors.

Despite the dire inevitability of his final illness, James handled it in his own way, never revealing much of his inner thoughts or feelings. He would talk about his "condition," but did not use the word, "cancer." He would try to create an atmosphere of optimism when we would visit him, talking about what he was planning to do "when I get out of here."

The last time that I visited him he came close to being open about his dire situation. His greeting to me as he forced a faint smile and offered a weak hand was, "Hello Brother Paul, shake hands with Brother Job."

A few months after James' death, I was visiting his wife Mary and she asked me if I would like to see the good-bye letter that he had written to his Momma. I was shocked. "Do you mean that the old boy finally came out of his shell and expressed himself?" I asked. "I sure would like to see that letter."

When I looked at the "letter," a short note on a piece of envelope, I cried as I was struck by the appropriateness of it. It was the perfect communication from the shy son who knew that he would never see his Momma again, and knew that she would understand the message just as she had understood him for forty-four years.

The note, unpunctuated and painfully printed in large capital letters with a hand attached to an arm broken as the result of bone cancer, and composed in a mind clouded by weeks of heavy pain-relieving medication, was as follows:

"HI MOM   FEEL BETTER NOW   BE HOME SOON - BAKE CORN BREAD & SOUR KRAUT   1 PC CRISP MEAT
*   BY-BY   JAMES"*

Principle No. 3. Set an example by walking humbly before God.

Leora, the third child, entered the family with a flourish. Dad would later say that May 4, 1929, was the busiest day of his life. He would say, "the day got started with Leora being born first thing in the morning and before the day was over an old cow had a calf, the sow had pigs, a settin' hen hatched, and the bees swarmed." I should get an old almanac and see what phase the moon was in that day.

Leora was 14 when her older brothers were drafted into military service and she and Rhodetta, aged 12, became Dad's farm hands. She took to this new responsibility very well. Even as a young teenager, she was strong and athletic. She was a legend at Griffith Creek Grade School, where she was one of the few people, male or female, who had ever hit a softball over the coal house in left field.

She and her sister took on the whole gamut of farming activities. Under Dad's watchful eye they planted, hoed, cut, shocked, and shucked the corn and hauled it into the crib. They helped him mow and rake the hay and put it into the barn until the barn was full and then they placed the rest around tall poles set into the ground, creating giant haystacks.

They followed Dad as he cradled the wheat and oats and they tied the grain into sheaves and shocked it, awaiting the arrival of the threshing machine. They helped feed the animals, milk the cows, and butcher the hogs. They cut, bladed, and topped the sorghum cane, then fed the stalks into the cane mill to extract the juice and kept the fire going under the evaporating pan until the ugly green juice had been transformed into beautiful amber molasses.

Since this was in the 1940's on a hillside farm in West Virginia, the horsepower on the farm was provided by, you guessed it, horses. Old John and Old Nell were our power sources, a team of gray, almost white, horses. Old Nell was the gentlest and smartest animal we ever had on the farm. She was so gentle that she could be safely ridden by the smallest child (that was me). She was so smart that there was no need for reins when she was pulling a cultivator. She knew just how to maneuver herself at the end of a corn row and she could turn to go in the opposite direction without stepping on a single stalk.

When I got old enough to work with Old Nell, I was constantly amazed by her intelligence and I would sometimes test her. I would put the chain around a hay shock to be pulled to the stack site and tell her to "git up" and then stand and watch as she would go directly to the stack site and stop at the perfect place for the hay to be pitched from the shock to the stack. She would then wait patiently for me to catch up and remove the chain and then she would go directly to another hay shock and position herself to pull it as soon as I had the chain in place.

It took Leora, though, to prove that Old Nell, in addition to being gentle and intelligent, had a well-developed sense of humor.

Early one summer morning, Leora and Rhodetta went on the daily ritual of getting the horses for the day's work. They found them in the pasture up the hollow from the barn. Leora, being the taller, had the job of putting the bridles on the horses. Her method was to speak to the horse, asking it to "bend down and open your mouth," in hopes that it would cooperate and make the task a bit easier.

After she had successfully bridled Old John and handed the reins to her sister, she bent over to pick up the bridle for Old Nell. Now Leora, as an adult woman, has always been slender and statuesque, but at age fifteen she was a bit heavier and I recall hearing her described as very "shapely." Evidently the sight before Old Nell was just too much even for a gentle, intelligent horse to overlook. She took one look at Leora's behind and then left big horse-tooth prints there as she took a generous bite out of those "tight-fittin'" jeans.

Leora was beautiful, smart, and ambitious. As soon as she graduated from high school, she went to Charleston and enrolled in a business college. I was impressed when she returned as a very stylish and sophisticated lady and certainly the most eligible young woman around. She began working in the First National Bank, in our town of Alderson, across the street from Lobban's Funeral Home. She had not worked there long until she was made aware, by all the talk from her circle of friends, that Charlie Lobban had a new assistant, and, boy-o-boy, was he good looking! Here she was, just across the street, and she was the last to find out about the new man in town.

Four months later, she became Mrs. Les Hunter.

Leora is the one of us that is the most like Momma. She cooks like Momma, works like Momma, prays like Momma, and represents Jesus in the world like Momma. She is apparently the latest in a line, for she inherited traits from Momma that Momma had inherited from her mother. Just as people in Grandma's time said that, "Uncle George is the preacher but Aunt Rhody is the saint," people in Momma's time called her a saint, and Leora has continued that legacy.

Her special calling from God has been to minister to the hopeless and helpless, the aged and the incurable. She has provided weeks, months, and even years of terminal care for close family members, distant family members, neighbors, and even those in desperate need that she had never met but had heard about. Her additional expressions of love through visitation, prayer, and sharing everything from the gospel to garden vegetables have helped hundreds of people.

Les was looking forward to his retirement so he and Leora could have more freedom to do the things that they had talked about over the years, but it did not work out that way. At the time of his retirement, Aunt Lura, one of Momma's surviving sisters was in dire straits. Aunt Lura was in her nineties, a widow who had outlived her son who was her only child, so she was all alone. Her eyesight had failed and she had recently fallen and broken her back.

So the first three years of Les' retirement were not spent in the nice new home he and Leora had built at Stanaford, instead they were spent in Aunt Lura's little house in Beckley as he and Leora locked up their home and moved in with Aunt Lura, caring for her until her death.

When Dad made out his final will, he wanted to keep the farm house and the original eighty-seven acres that he and Momma had bought in 1925 identified with the Dodd name so he distributed his other land and possessions to the rest of the family and left me, his only surviving son, the "home place."

For someone who lived six hundred miles away, taking care of the "home place" can be very frustrating and guilt producing. At first I rented the house and then left it empty for awhile, getting there to see about it every six months, or so.

Then one day shortly after Aunt Lura's death as Rose and I were visiting Les and Leora in their home, I asked Les what or who would be Leora's next project. "What she wants to do now," Les said, "is to buy an old farmhouse out in the country somewhere and fix it up."

"Don't buy one," I responded, "let me give you one."

"I heard that," Leora said as she quickly came from the kitchen where she and Rose had been visiting, "and I accept."

Boy, did I make a good deal that day. For the price of a hug from a grateful sister, I transferred ownership of the farmhouse and five acres to her and Les, gained freedom from the guilt I was suffering for not keeping the property up, and then had the pleasure of watching them, in a true labor of love, restore and improve the "home place." It now serves as a second home for them, and they especially like to get "snowed in" away from the rest of the world during the winter. In the summer, they grow the flowers that Momma grew.

The house looks and smells like it did when Momma was there, especially after Leora has cooked up one of her big dinners. We have been able to host family reunions there which have been attended not only by family but also by neighbors and friends from bygone days.

Where did Leora learn these traits of unconditional love, empathy for the suffering, concern for the forgotten, and finding joy and fulfillment in humble service to those who cannot repay?

She learned them from Momma. From her infancy she, like the rest of us, went with Momma and saw her visit the lonely, comfort the suffering, and share our meager possessions with those in need. She saw Momma demonstrate that there was no person, regardless of the person's condition or position, who was not worthy of her tender concern and care. She followed Jesus by patterning her life of service after his, and thus, provided a pattern for her daughter.

"Leora came at noon. We went over to see about Ethel in the afternoon"
Momma's diary: November 7, 1959

Principle No. 4. Encourage children to let their lights shine - for God's glory.

There is usually a star performer in a family and, sure enough, our family had one. Rhodetta entered the world with unlimited dreams, ideas, ambition, and talent. Her creativity showed up early in life. Before she was six years old she was convinced that she could not be a true member of such a mundane family so, therefore, she must have been adopted.

When she was scolded she would go around the house and pout beside the large stone chimney, thinking of the sympathy she would get if only the chimney would fall on her. As she got older, Leora swore that every time it was Rhodetta's turn to wash the dishes, she would get an uncontrollable urge to go to the toilet. And she would go there and stay there, and stay there.

And expressive? Boy, was she. I remember one incident when she and I were walking down the road with Momma and Dad to Uncle Larry's house when I was about four and she was about ten. Something had evidently happened, or didn't happen, to her satisfaction and I remember Dad saying as she walked briskly on ahead of us, "She's the only young-un I ever saw that you can tell how mad she is by looking at the back of her head."

How did Momma react to this budding superstar in the family? She encouraged, she taught, and she empowered Rhodetta. She taught her what she could about playing on our old pump organ. She taught her to sing harmony. She and Dad arranged for her to take piano lessons which she started on the old organ, and then bought her a second-hand piano. Momma shared with her the mysteries of crocheting, embroidery, quilt making, sewing, and all the other skills that she knew. And Momma strove mightily to teach her one other thing: a person's gifts and talents come from the Lord and are to be used to glorify him.

By the time Rhodetta was a young teenager, her creative skills were taking her far beyond Momma's very practical approach to things. Momma would make a quilt for its comfort; Rhodetta would make one for its beauty. Momma would make a dress to wear around the house; Rhodetta would make a dress to make a fashion statement. Momma would play an old hymn on the piano; Rhodetta was graduating into the highbrow stuff.

Although I was six years younger than Rhodetta, we had a few conflicts. If I had been smart, I would have left her alone when she was in one of her "creative" moments. I remember once when she was about twelve or thirteen, she was sewing something on Momma's old treadle sewing machine and I kept pestering her until she told me, "get out of here or I am going to slap you down a rat hole." I thought that this was serious enough to call to Momma's attention, but when I told her of Rhodetta's unspeakable cruelty to me she just quietly said, "you should leave your sister alone."

I was perfectly willing to take Momma's advice, just as soon as I got in a parting shot, so I wandered back into the sewing area of Momma's bedroom and very calmly and matter-of-factly told Rhodetta that I wished she was dead. Rhodetta now thought that this was serious enough to call to Momma's attention and Momma thought that this was serious enough to get out the heavy wooden paddle that she used to stir laundry, and gave me a serious spanking.

I learned my lesson well. Momma had just shown me why it is not acceptable to wish that someone was dead, so I knew that I would never do that again, and I haven't. So, as soon as my sobbing had subsided enough for me to talk, I returned to the sewing area and more correctly informed Rhodetta that I wished that she had never been born. Momma did not like that statement any better than the first one and here came the wooden paddle again. Have you ever had blisters added to your bruises? I don't know if I had blistered bruises or bruised blisters, but I do know that I finally got the whole message.

Momma got real worried when, at age sixteen, Rhodetta fell head-over-heels for a young man named Ralph Jones who was a local country music personality. Ralph had his own band and a radio show and made personal appearances around the area. Once, when Bill Monroe and the Bluegrass Boys came to Hinton, Ralph played the fiddle with them in their performance.

Ralph was just as creative and ambitious as Rhodetta, but what bothered Momma was that she was afraid that his ambition was more Nashville-centered than Heaven-centered. Rhodetta was clever, though. When she sang on Ralph's radio program, she always chose to be a part of the obligatory religious song that closed the show.

It was soon obvious that Ralph and Rhodetta were made for each other; obvious, that is, to everyone but Momma and Dad. Momma felt better after Ralph told her of his conversion experience but Dad didn't. Dad got busy and did a little bit of research on his own. One day when he was in Hinton, he decided he would stop into O. R. Grimmett Motors where Ralph was working as a mechanic.

Evidently Ralph had just dropped a tool on his toe or something equally upsetting, because Dad announced at supper that night that he had "never heard a worse bunch of words come out of a man's mouth, and then he saw me." It should not have come as a shock to anyone that when Ralph asked Dad for his permission to marry Rhodetta, Dad turned him down flat.

When Rhodetta informed Momma that she and Ralph were making plans to "run away" and get married anyway, Momma relented and went with them to Hinton and gave her permission for the wedding license to be issued.

The big question now was, what was Dad going to do? We did not know until an hour before the wedding if he was even going to attend the ceremony or not. He did finally decide to go, but did not participate except to sob loudly through the entire ceremony. (Incidentally, he had treated Leora in the very same way. He said that there was just something about giving up his daughters that "got to him." He grinned broadly through all of his son's weddings.)

For whatever reason, and it was probably because of Momma's prayers and constant reminders, Rhodetta has used her many talents to glorify God. She works in her church's music program as accompanist and choir director and Ralph sits on the front row of the church so they can sit together during the sermon. At Christmas and Easter, she organizes and leads a combined choir from three or four rural churches in a cantata or other presentation which she creates. She takes a group from her church to sing at the nursing home every week.

She and Ralph have a museum in their house which they proudly share with anyone who wants to see it. Their museum covers American Indian culture and pioneer days up to the era in which they were born. When asked, Rhodetta puts on her Indian outfit and goes to local schools or other gatherings and, after showing them a picture of our Indian ancestor, educates them about Indian life and customs.

At other times, she puts on her old long dress, bonnet, and shawl and fills up a wash tub with things from another era and demonstrates what life was like before the advent of modern miracles like machines and electricity. She was sure that she was getting through to her audiences until one day, after she had spent an hour educating a third and fourth grade group by telling them story after story, all of which she knew to be true, Ralph heard one boy say to another as they were leaving, "I don't believe a word of what that old woman said."

Rhodetta, Ralph, Judy, Eugene, and Mary Carol came. I was expecting them (just a little). Rhodetta brought a beautiful cake with candles and "Happy Birthday" on it. Rhodetta and Rosie served cake, coffee and RC so we had a real pleasant evening together."
Momma's diary: January 2, 1959

Principle 5. Do not let the children get between Momma and Dad.

"Argue, argue, argue! All you ever do is argue! Boy, you would argue with a stump!" was an indictment which I heard more than once from Dad.

Dad was a very intelligent person and well informed but, somehow, he and I seemed to disagree over a lot of things. Not all of our arguments ended in a stalemate. I never won one of them, but he often did, and some of them he won even by his power of persuasion.

During the Korean War, I was outraged when President Harry Truman fired General Douglas MacArthur merely because the general insisted on carrying on the war the way he wanted to and started moving across the Yalu River into Manchuria/China. General MacArthur was one of my heroes and I had a large picture of West Point on the wall of my room and President Truman was one of the most unpopular presidents of all time, so I loudly voiced my support for the members of Congress who were promising to impeach the president for this dastardly act.

"Son," Dad patiently (very unusual for him) said, "this country is based on some important principles and one of them is that the president is the Commander-in-Chief of the Army, and just like the people serving under General MacArthur have to obey his orders even if they don't like 'em, General MacArthur has to obey the president's orders. He was in the process of disobeying orders so President Truman didn't have a choice. He had to fire him."

I was not convinced at the time that the best military strategy was being followed, but I eventually came to the conclusion that the right action had been taken by a person who would eventually be recognized as a great and courageous president.

Another lesson I learned from Dad was during the driest summer we ever had. The pasture was brown, the corn stunted, and the creeks had dried up, and it seemed like it would never rain again. "Boy, are we stupid," I opined from my vast teen-aged wisdom, "farming is no way to make a living, it is no better than gambling."

"No, son," Dad explained, not patiently, but forcefully, "farming is not like gambling at all. Farming is a contract between man and God. We are expected to plow, plant, and cultivate and then trust God for the increase."

Okay! So maybe Dad did know a few things that I didn't but he could still be infuriating because he was like a rock, stubborn, and with a firm opinion about everything.

Momma, by contrast, seemed to be soft and always ready to hear another point of view and give a measure of agreement, even to some of my radical ideas. So it was natural that when I hit a stone wall (Dad), I would turn to Momma for understanding and support. Once, when I was in my mid-teens and Dad and I had reached loggerheads on some issue, I took my frustration and absolutely air-tight logic to Momma, fully expecting that she would be able to talk some sense into my totally wrong and unreasonable father.

Instead, she patiently explained "Principle Five" to me. "Honey," she said, "I understand what you are saying, and you may be right. But I also have heard your Dad's side and I don't think that he is all wrong. Please don't ask me to take sides between the two of you, for if I have to take sides, I will choose your Dad."

"What?" I thought. "How can this be? I am so logical and lovable and Dad is so stubborn and wrong." I do not remember the words that I used to express my outrage for her not coming to my defense, but she just calmly continued her explanation.

"For one thing," she said, "he is your father. He is a very smart man, and you need to respect him. For another, in a few years you will leave us and be out on you own, but your Dad and I will be together for the rest of our lives. Even though we sometimes disagree on things, we have always supported each other when it came to raising you kids."

I have thought a lot about this concept. Many times since then I have seen marriages get into trouble and even fall apart because parents let children come between them. A child who is given greater consideration than a good and faithful parent by a well-meaning but doting other parent is given more power than he or she should have. That was a lesson that I needed to learn and Momma gave it to me straight. It made me mad, though, but she taught me.

"Jan. 2 is my 62nd birthday. Paul started back to college about 9 this morn. I hated for him to leave as I always miss him so much."
Momma's diary: January 2, 1958

"Jan. 2nd, 1963, My 67th Birthday. I am very thankful to God for letting me live to have another Birthday. He has been so very

merciful and good to me each year of my life. I fear my life hasn't amounted to very much for Him, but I have tried to be faithful.

I hope to be more faithful in His service the remaining days or years of my life I am so thankful for my dear Companion, Arthur, who has always been patient, loving and kind to me. May God continue to bless and comfort his dear heart always.

Our dear precious children (Arthur Jr., James, Leora, Rhodetta, Paul), their dear companions, and our sweet grandchildren are all so precious to our hearts. Only God knows how much love is in my heart for each one. My daily prayer is that we well be an unbroken family around God's blessed throne.

God wants to save us all through His matchless, everlasting love."
Handwritten page, folded and filed in old Bible

I hope that it is evident to you that the five principles which I chose to elaborate on are but the tip of an iceberg. Momma fulfilled her contract with God as fully as was possible. I saved one other principle for a whole chapter for itself. Principle Six has to be: Tell them the stories of Jesus.

8 TELL THEM THE STORIES OF JESUS, OR DON'T JUST WASTE TIME IRONING

"Eternal Life through Jesus Christ is the greatest gift thatanyone can receive."
Written by Momma on the blank page in the front of her diary, as underlined by Momma.

By the time I was six years old I had a degree in theology, from the College of Momma.

Every Tuesday was ironing day and, in my preschool years, that was my favorite day of the week, especially during the winter. Although she had a perfectly good ironing board, Momma chose to iron on the kitchen table, which suited me fine.

Since she used black flatirons which were heated on the wood-burning cook stove, this meant that the kitchen was toasty warm on those cold winter Tuesdays and, since my brothers and sisters were at school and Dad was at the Alderson Livestock Market where he worked every Tuesday as clerk for the livestock auction, I had Momma all to myself. I would park myself on the bench behind the table and ask her to tell me stories.

What Momma told me were Bible stories. Although I have lived many years, done considerable study, and seen numerous dramatic portrayals of these same stories, the details and images which are a part of my mind still come from those stories which she told me.

Even today, when I read, or hear a sermon, about little Samuel being taken by Hannah, his mother, to live in the Temple with Eli, the priest, I have a feeling of anxiety and separation due to the clear picture which I formed as a child about that event.

Samuel looks just like me, Hannah looks just like Momma, and

Eli looks just like our pastor at the time, Brother Earl Ward. When Samuel heard God's voice, he was sleeping on the front pew of the Griffith Creek Baptist Church, and he then quickly ran to the back pew to wake up Eli/Brother Ward to get advice. Only after Eli explained it to him did Samuel realize that it was the voice of God coming down from the belfry directly above the pulpit.

When Momma described how Adam and Eve were expelled from the Garden of Eden, I pictured the two angels with flaming swords standing under the big mulberry trees in our back yard, guarding the gate to Momma's vegetable garden to prevent Adam and Eve from reentering Eden.

When I hear about the faithful father watching and waiting for the return of his prodigal son, I remember Dad standing on our front porch looking down the road toward Route 3, hoping to see someone in a sailor's uniform walking toward our house after one of his sons had written and said that he may have enough leave to come home for a few days even in the midst of the war.

I had no doubts about the ability of Noah to build the ark. Noah, to me, was our neighbor, Noah Flint, who lived on top of the mountain on a beautiful farm which adjoined our place. Mr. Flint's house and buildings were far away from the public eye, nearly two miles from the highway, but the trip to his homestead was worth it. His house, his barn, and his outbuildings were like something from a magazine.

He had been born in the same house where I was born, but that was many years before Dad had bought the place from the Flint family. When Noah had become an adult, he had selected his farm and the site for his home from some of the large acreage which his family owned.

He had personally designed and built all of the structures on his farm. His house had a wrap-around porch which afforded a breathtaking view of the beautiful Greenbrier River valley with the town of Alderson clearly visible three or four miles away. His buildings were functional but also unique as they were adorned with cupolas, weather vanes, and lightning rods, and equipped with every convenience that pre-electricity mechanical advantage could provide. The rainwater which fell on these buildings was captured by roof gutters and piped into a cistern which supplied the water for the farm.

The Noah that I knew was a builder, a craftsman, and an inventor. He designed a porch swing with a treadle which propelled it, making swinging even more fun for a little boy. He had a complete blacksmith shop which I found fascinating, especially when he would let me turn the crank on the bellows to heat up the coals in the forge.

He did not put his hay into the barn with sweat and a pitchfork like we did, he put the hay into his barn mechanically by inserting a large hay fork into a wagon load of hay and then pulled it up into his barn with his tractor by means of a rope attached to the fork.

He did woodworking, metalworking, carpentry, blacksmithing, farming, orcharding, you name it, he could do it. And besides all that he was a church leader and red-hot politician with a smile and personality very much like that of his hero, Franklin Delano Roosevelt.

Build an ark? Of course, Noah could build an ark. Noah could do anything.

A few years ago, Noah Flint's daughter, Imogene, related a great story to me about her family. She told about how her father kept teasing her mother about cooking him a groundhog. Now a groundhog was a plentiful, perfectly clean, vegetation-eating little animal that not only predicted the weather every February second, but also provided a very tasty main course on the tables of many of the Flint's neighbors, especially during hard times. Nevertheless, Mrs. Ida Flint wanted no part of it. After a while, though, she became tired of Noah's teasing and agreed to cook one of the despised rodents only if he would skin and clean it and not expect her or their two dainty little girls to eat any of it.

Their youngest daughter, Ophelia, had other ideas, though. She was five years old and not about to let her father eat something (and brag about it excessively) without having a taste for herself. So, to her mother's chagrin, Ophelia joined her father in the feast.

After the meal, Mrs. Flint swore the whole family to secrecy. "I don't want any of you to ever tell anybody that we ate a groundhog," was her stern order.

"Yes, Momma," was the obedient reply from Imogene and Ophelia.

On Saturday, they went into Alderson for their weekly shopping and, as usual, stopped in John Alderson's ladies apparel store where a relative worked. "Ophelia," the relative gushed as she took the little girl into her arms and hugged her, "You are so pretty. What do you eat that makes you so pretty?"

"Groundhog!" was Ophelia's instant response, given as her mother desperately tried to get her hand over the little girl's mouth.

Noah Flint was a Democrat. Not just a Democrat, he was a "red-hot" Democrat, a Democrat through and through. Even though I knew him in the 1940's and 50's, he still had an "Al Smith For President" sign hanging in his workshop. He was a great political story teller and Imogene's story reminded me of one he told me which also involved a groundhog. In 1952, just after Dwight D. Eisenhower, a Republican, was elected President, he told me that as soon as one old groundhog had heard the election results, he began working frantically, digging his hole much deeper. The younger groundhogs asked him why he was doing this. "Well," he told them, "my great-great-great grandfather had a hole six feet deep when Hoover was President and they dug him out."

Samson was my brother, James. As Momma would tell me about Samson's great strength and feats of valor, I would picture him accomplishing great things with the same speed and energy with which James overpowered tasks.

James, like Samson was unbelievably strong, even as a teenager. I had no doubt that he could kill lions with his bare hands. He worked one summer for a neighbor, Earl Bowden, who drilled water wells. Earl told Dad that on James' first day at work, he pointed out to James a length of well casing that needed to be moved from one place to another and when he returned, the casing had been moved. When he asked how it got there, James told him that he had picked it up and carried it. Was that not what he wanted him to do? Earl then told him that he did not intend for him to move it himself, he wanted it moved when the rest of the crew got there, because lifting a casing of that size was a four-man job.

David was a fascinating character to me. I had no trouble picturing him, sunburned, freckle-faced, barefoot, and wearing bib overalls with no shirt, killing Goliath with his slingshot and a Griffith Creek rock until Momma told me that his slingshot was not like mine. Every boy of my day had a slingshot, or "gravel-shooter." These were made with a forked stick with two strong prongs from which to tie strips of an old inner tube with a pocket in back to hold and launch the ammunition. From the earliest age every boy's eyes were trained to look for the ideally symmetrical Y-shaped fork in a small tree which would make the perfect slingshot. Even before the boy could be trusted with a knife, he would locate the perfect fork and get his father, brother, or other older person to cut it for him.

So when Momma told me that David's slingshot was made entirely without wood, I was baffled. Even after she described what his slingshot looked like and how it worked, I could not figure it out. So then she took me out to the smokehouse where the old shoes were kept, and she cut the tongue out of one of them, used an awl to punch a hole in each end of the tongue, and tied a piece of rawhide thong into each hole and presented me with a genuine, honest-to-goodness, Biblically-correct, sanctified slingshot.

Now my respect for David climbed to new heights. I was a pretty good shot with my "gravel-shooter" but I could not, literally, hit the side of the barn with my new sanctified model. First, I would put a stone in the tongue/pocket and it would fall out. Although I did not doubt Momma's explanation of how centrifugal force works, it took a lot of practice to get it to work for me. I understood the principal for I had often seen my older brothers take a full bucket of milk and "show off" by turning it over and over in a big windmill motion without spilling a drop.

Finally I mastered the art of keeping the rock in the pocket of the slingshot while I whirled it around and around my head, but that is where my skill ended. When I would release one of the thongs and hurl the rock, it was as likely to hit something directly behind me as to hit something in front of me. If I ever hit within ten feet of a target, it was mere chance. Poor David! Out there fighting lions and giant Philistines without the benefit of modern implements of war, without even a forked stick or strips of an inner tube for his slingshot.

I loved the stories of the friendship between David and Jonathan. I have been fortunate to have had a number of "Jonathans" in my life, and the model of their friendship described by Momma has served me well.

She also told me about King David sitting on his roof and watching a woman take a bath. She did not have to convince me that this was a bad thing to do. At age four or five, I could not think of anything more disgusting than that.

The bigger lesson that Momma drove home with that story was that one bad thing just leads to another. Just as Momma taught that one puff or one drink can lead to greater problems, she taught that one little sin and one little lie can lead to a bigger sin and a bigger lie and before long some serious sinning with dire consequences will be taking place.

Looking led to taking, taking led to lying, and lying led to killing. In this story, she taught me that David, even though he was "a man after God's own heart," was not the hero; the prophet Nathan who risked his life by confronting David with his sins was the hero and David could not resume his role as the hero until he had repented and paid a great price for his sin.

When I read or hear the story of "the three Hebrew children" in the fiery furnace, I have to force myself to visualize a domed brick kiln or other logical "fiery furnace" that would have been used at that time and place.

My natural inclination is to see a gigantic version of a coal burning furnace which looks like the one used to heat the Johnson and Gwinn Hardware store in Alderson when I was young. I see shovel full after shovel full of coal being loaded into the huge door as the furnace is heated hotter and hotter. Then after Shadrach, Meshach, and Abednego are stuffed in through the door of the furnace and the observers look in, the fourth person that they see in the fire doesn't just look like the Son of God, he is the Son of God, because that is the way Momma told me the story.

In all likelihood, modern Christian educators would not agree with Momma's method of giving out the complete story on some of the events in the Bible to someone as young as her children were when she began teaching us. Today's Sunday School teachers who work with the younger classes are discouraged from discussing the gory details of some of the Biblical accounts since it is assumed that children could not understand them and would be traumatized.

I do not know for sure how I feel about this but two things do jump out at me; first, I do not believe that I was traumatized beyond repair by hearing about the crucifixion of Jesus, the beheading of John the Baptist, or the stoning death of Stephen, and second, if we take a look at the stuff that kids are shown on television and choose to watch, Hollywood may know something we have missed.

In her telling of Bible stories to me, Momma took me to the Garden of Eden where she introduced me to sin entering the world and taught me that sin has terrible and far-reaching consequences. She took me to the flood and introduced me to Noah and his family and taught me that God punishes sin but always makes a way of escape for his faithful people. She introduced me to Abraham and explained how God called him and used him to be the father of a great nation, God's chosen people. She took me from Abraham to Isaac to Jacob to Joseph and the time of slavery into Egypt.

She described to me how Moses' mother had made a basket of reeds, put the baby Moses into it and then set him afloat in the Greenbrier, oops, Nile River where he was watched by his sister, Leora, oops, Miriam and then he was rescued and raised by Pharaoh's daughter. She made the plagues real - the frogs, locusts, hail, fire, and especially the Passover where the households which were protected by the blood of the lamb did not suffer the loss of their firstborn sons.

The parting of the sea, the forty years in the wilderness, the Ten Commandments and the golden calf, the pillar of fire, the manna, and the unwillingness of the people to go into the Promised Land were used by Momma to illustrate God's love and faithfulness and the great price we pay when our lives fall short of God's purpose for us.

I did not fully appreciate the miracle of Moses getting water out of a rock, because I was familiar with water coming from that source. Our water supply was a spring which came out of a small rock cave at the base of the mountain about fifty yards from our house. Just as in Moses' time, water coming out of a rock is a true gift from God. Sparkling, pure, clear, cold water is a great blessing and the Lord doubly blessed us because the elevation of the spring was higher than our house, which gave Dad a great idea.

Long before we had electricity needed for a water pump to provide water pressure, Dad decided to put "water in the house," taking advantage of gravity flow from the spring. He raised the elevation of the water by eighteen inches by building a small concrete dam at the spring opening. He then put in the pipe and ran the water into the kitchen.

Our cook stove, known to Dad but unknown to the rest of us, was equipped with fittings where a water line could be connected so when Momma was cooking, the stove would heat water which was then stored in a cylindrical tank we placed between the stove and the sink. It wasn't pretty, but it sure was functional.

The short portion of our L-shaped back porch was enclosed, a tub, sink, and commode were installed and wonder of wonders, we had ourselves an indoor bathroom. Without knowing how big to make it, we probably made the biggest single dwelling septic tank on record.

Dad then cut large sandstone rocks and replaced the old wooden springhouse with a permanent stone and concrete building. He even formed and poured a concrete roof on the new structure. Cold water coming from the rock, protected by an enclosure of eight inch thick stone walls, created a wonderful place for storing milk, butter, cottage cheese, or one of Momma's banana filled cakes on a hot summer's day and it was the best place ever invented for cooling a watermelon.

Momma, through her stories, took me to the manger in Bethlehem, to the Temple with Jesus when he was twelve, through his ministry with the miracles and teachings, and on to Gethsemane and Calvary. I still remember the sadness in Momma's voice as she told me many times about Jesus in Gethsemane asking three disciples to watch with him, and upon finding them asleep saying, "could ye not watch with me one hour?"

She took me beyond the cross, to the empty tomb, to the risen Lord, to his appearances to his followers, and to his ascent into heaven. And she did not stop there. I think her favorite story ended with her quoting, "Ye men of Galilee, why stand ye gazing up into heaven? This same Jesus, which is taken up from you into heaven, shall so come in like manner as ye have seen him go into heaven."

She lived every day of her life looking forward to that event - his return.

9 PRAY WITHOUT CEASING, OR NEVER STOP PRAYING

"I am so thankful for my dear companion who has been very sweet and kind through the years, for my children, in-laws, and grandchildren. All are very precious. My daily prayer is that each one will be saved by accepting Jesus as their own personal Savior."
Momma's diary: January 2, 1959, on her sixty-third birthday

Momma not only told us Bible stories, she also lived out the message of the stories in front of us.

The prophet Daniel was a particularly compelling model for her. No, I am not saying that she crawled into any lion's dens, although God's loving watch care over her for eighty years undoubtedly involved closing the mouths of some formidable lions, but the aspect of Daniel which she admired and sought to emulate was his prayer life.

Daniel prayed to God three times a day, she told us, even after a royal decree was written which made prayer to anyone other than King Darius a crime punishable by becoming lion food. After the decree, Momma said, Daniel not only continued to pray three times a day, he went upstairs and opened the window and prayed in plain view where everyone could see and hear him. I think that Daniel's boldness fit well with Momma's own commitment to serve God completely in spite of external conditions or distractions. It also fit well with the emphasis on holiness which she had been taught by her parents.

Momma knew that there were at least two ways of interpreting I Thessalonians 5:17, which reads, "Pray without ceasing." The first interpretation to which she ascribed was "pray all the time," and it appeared to me that she did that. In any situation or setting when I was near her, I was never surprised to hear her breathing a prayer. Sometimes is was a prayer of thanks, sometimes a prayer of intercession, or sometimes a prayer of praise. She even ended her yawns as bedtime approached with a soft "thank you, dear Lord," as she neared the close of the constant conscious communication which she and her Heavenly Father had experienced throughout the day.

She also knew that "pray without ceasing." could be interpreted, "never stop praying," or "never give up praying," because God rewards the faith that is proven by persistent prayer. She would continue to pray for a person or matter for years, demonstrating her belief in the faithfulness of God and his promises. Just as her mother, before her, had prayed without ceasing for her children and step children, that they might all be saved and united around God's throne, Momma also prayed without ceasing for her ever increasing family of children, in-laws, grandchildren, and great-grandchildren that we, also, might be an unbroken circle in heaven.

Let me take you through one of Momma's typical days (with a few digressions and diversions, of course).

Getting up time was early in the morning, usually around 5:30. Dad would arise and first replenish the fire in the fireplace (or the stove which eventually replaced the fireplace) in the living room if the weather was cold. He would then build a fire in the cook stove in the kitchen. As soon as Dad was up, Momma would kneel beside the bed and begin her day on her knees in prayer. I can picture that scene from my earliest memories; Momma, her hair hanging down long and unbraided, with her bare feet showing under the hem of her flannel nightgown as she knelt on both knees and prayed softly, starting a new day of constant communication with her Heavenly Father.

By the time Dad had the fires going and his hired hands (that was us) up and ready to go out and do the milking, feeding and other farm chores, Momma had dressed, braided her hair, and was ready to take on the day. Her prayer life did not stop when she hit the kitchen and began making oatmeal, frying ham or tender loin or sausage, stirring up biscuits, perking coffee, making gravy, and whatever else she was going to serve us for breakfast. As she prepared breakfast, she always communicated with God through songs of worship and praise. Two of the songs which she sang every morning were ones she had learned almost as soon as she had learned to talk. They were familiar to her from her earliest days in a Godly home and in her church.

She would sing:

"Praise God, from whom all blessings flow;
Praise Him, all creatures here below;
Praise Him above, ye heavenly host;
Praise Father, Son, and Holy Ghost. Amen"

And then she would sing:

"Glory be to the Father, and to the Son, and to the Holy Ghost;
As it was in the beginning,
Is now and ever shall be,
World without end. Amen. Amen."

I know that in some churches these songs, the Doxology and the Gloria Patri, have been relegated to the archives. I have heard people say that they are just ritual songs and have no meaning, and besides that, a praise song has to have a beat that you can get excited about. Whoever heard of clapping your hands to the Doxology or the Gloria Patri? Just try it. It doesn't work. How can they be good praise songs?

I am in a church which sings one or the other of these songs every week, and when I am at the piano it is my privilege to play them, and let me assure you that neither of these songs will ever represent anything to me other than heartfelt praise to God, honoring him as highly as human language permits.

We would complete the chores in an hour or so and sit down to breakfast. Dad would ask the blessing in a droning, almost sing-song fashion, using the same blessing and tone that his father had used. He would begin strong and his voice would gradually soften until he concluded the prayer with a whispered "amen."

"Heavenly Father, we thank you for the preservation of our lives through the night, and for this morning's refreshment. Bless this food to the nourishment of our bodies, and our souls to thy service. In Jesus' name. Amen."

I do not know if Momma could have quoted Dad's blessing because while he was praying, she did not appear to be listening. Her lips would be moving slightly as, I assume, she was also thanking God for the food. She did not have to thank God for "preservation of her life through the night," she had already taken care of that an hour earlier.

By 7:15 a. m. (or was it 7:30? I am not sure), Momma would have the kitchen cleaned up and most of us would be out of the house and she would go into the living room and sit by the radio. There she would listen to "The Nation's Family Prayer Period," from the Cadle Tabernacle in Indianapolis, Indiana, a fifteen minute broadcast over WLW, Cincinnati, Ohio. The program always began with Mrs. Cadle's gentle vibrato singing, "Ere you left your room this morning, did you think to pray?" No wonder Momma liked that program. She was on the same wave length with them.

After the opening theme song, a few remarks, and another song by Mrs. Cadle or Richard Ford, E. Howard Cadle, the founder of the Tabernacle and radio program would give a short devotional sermon which not only helped Momma, it helped hundreds of thousands within the listening area of that powerful station get their day started off on a solid spiritual foundation.

When E. Howard Cadle died, he was replaced as Tabernacle pastor and radio speaker by a flamboyant West Virginian, Dr. B. R. Lakin. Dr. Lakin's messages were always very spiritual, serious, and to the point, just like Rev. Cadle's had been. Momma liked that kind of messages.

Dr. Lakin also continued Rev. Cadle's tradition of flying around the country and conducting "one-night revivals." I was about twelve years old when we heard that Dr. Lakin was bringing his "one-night revival" to our own Summers County Memorial Building in Hinton. Of course, we went; Momma, Dad, and I.

Momma had heard from someone that, in his personal appearances, Dr. Lakin was quite an entertainer and somewhat different than the very serious devotion leader that he was on the radio program. That someone was right! He was more fun than a circus.

He told about the little boy who yelled to the atheist lecturer, "You are dumber than a fool!" "Why would you say that, little boy?" the atheist asked. "Because the Bible says that 'the fool has said in his heart, there is no God,' but you done spit it out of your mouth," was the boy's reply.

Dr. Lakin talked about "stiff, sourpuss Christians who had consecration confused with constipation." "They don't need more of the Holy Spirit," he thundered, "what they need a good dose of Carter's

Little Liver Pills."

He went on this way for about an hour, and before the audience had the tears of laughter wiped from their eyes, the choir began singing, "Just As I Am," and people began flocking to the front of the auditorium. I went out of the Memorial Building thinking that this had been the greatest night of my life. We had been entertained by the best live show I had ever seen and then nearly a hundred people went to the front to get saved. Wow! That is the way to conduct a revival!

Momma saw the night's events a little differently than I did, however. Although she still listened to him on "The Nation's Family Prayer Period," I do not believe she ever got over her feeling that Dr. Lakin had largely wasted a "sacred opportunity" telling jokes and "bordering on blackguard" when he could have been making a more serious presentation of the gospel.

Before I go on with a typical day, I need to describe the radio that she listened to prior to the coming of electricity to our house. We had a large table model Zenith battery-powered radio. During World War II batteries, like everything else, were scarce so Dad wired our radio so it could be powered by an automobile battery. He then connected a small generator to the gasoline motor of Momma's Sears-Roebuck washing machine which then recharged the battery every Monday as Momma did the laundry. This worked great except when the radio was played too much during the week and we could barely hear Jack Benny on Sunday night.

"It has been a busy day. I always take time to read a chapter and pray before starting my work which gives me a good start for the day. I skimmed the milk, defrosted the refrigerator, cleaned up the house, and cut up a coon to freeze before noon."
Momma's diary: October 24, 1958

Returning to Momma's day, as soon as the radio program was over, she spent a time of Bible reading and serious prayer. I think that this corresponded to Daniel's first prayer of the day. After our noon meal and we had scattered, she again spent time with her Bible and in prayer.

"It has been a nice day but still rather cold; six above zero. We

have a good fire and enjoying the evening reading and listening to the
radio. Will soon have our worship period."
Momma's diary, February 10, 1958

Before bedtime each night, the radio would be turned off and Momma, after offering to let Dad do it, which he always politely declined, would read a passage from the Bible aloud and then kneel at her rocking chair and pour out her heart to God. She did not leave anything out. She always began her prayer by praising and glorifying her Heavenly Father and by giving thanks for his blessings.

She would then pray for each of us by name with specific spiritual and physical requests to God for us. She would go up and down the road of our community praying for the various needs of our neighbors. She would pray for our church, our pastor, other church leaders, and other churches. She would pray for missionaries and Rescue Missions.

She would pray for the President, regardless of Dad's political opinion of the White House occupant at the time. She would pray for other world leaders, always praying for peace. She would pray for all of "our soldier boys" around the world. And she would pray for the lost and weep as she pled with God to draw them to him "before it is eternally too late."

By the time she got down to asking for a good night's rest and God's protection over us we knew that Momma's prayer was coming to an end and we could soon go to bed. But I do not think that any of us ever went to bed without the assurance that God had his eye on our home and that he had just had an extended conversation with one of his "good and faithful servants."

For a long time after Momma's death, I felt like I was in "free-fall" because Momma was not here to pray for me. Only after she was gone did I realize how much I had relied on that which I had taken for granted. Only after they were no longer there did I fully appreciate Momma's ceaseless prayers.

10 SING PRAISES TO THE LORD, RIGHT AFTER YOU TESTIFY

"Sing praises to God, sing praises: sing praises unto our King, sing praises."

Psalms 47: 6

Momma was perfectly in tune with the Psalmist because she, too, believed in worshipping God by singing. Momma's taste in music began and ended with the music which glorified God, and worship through music was a very defining part of who she was. As previously mentioned, she began each day praising God with the Doxology and Gloria Patri, and she and Dad first developed interest in each other while singing together in a volunteer choir at a neighbor's wake.

Music was the gateway to Momma's soul. Many years ago, Arthur, Jr. gave her an album of songs by the Vaughn Quartet which were precious to her. I can still see her sitting beside the old Victrola listening to their beautiful, complex arrangement of "O, Happy Day," and having an ecstatic experience in the Lord, crying and rejoicing.

Momma had an overwhelming desire to share her faith with others. She demonstrated, to all who knew her, God's love and compassion by her actions. She taught her children and those in her various Sunday School classes the stories of Jesus, but it seemed to her never to be enough. I have always believed that she was stymied by her culture which prevented her from becoming a preacher.

The Methodist culture of the early 1900's in which she was raised and her Baptist culture of the middle of the century both discouraged, or flatly forbade, women in the preaching ministry. She got as close as she could by teaching, testifying, leading devotional services, leading in congregational prayer, and using any other avenue of sharing her faith that was available to her.

I often sensed her frustration, and she would occasionally wonder aloud if she could have served God better if she had become a foreign missionary instead of marrying and raising a family. In some strange, twisted, elitist way, her religious culture approved of women preaching the gospel to foreigners, but not to Americans.

Following one of Dad's numerous "life-threatening episodes," I asked Momma what she would do if Dad preceded her in death. She did not hesitate. She said that she would go to Charleston and work at Pat Withrow's Union Mission. She had never been to a Rescue Mission and maybe had never been to Charleston, but she did know that there would always be an opportunity for her to do God's work by helping others.

Music was Momma's open door. Music was one way in which she could share the gospel, even from the pulpit to an entire congregation. Give her an opportunity to sing before a crowd and she was there. And music was not all you got, either. She never sang without first giving a sermon, oops, testimony, in some way urging all listeners to completely surrender their lives to the Lord.

I must have come along about the time that music began to take a larger place in our family's life. Evidently, the life of a struggling family in the depths of the Great Depression did not leave much time for music, nor, maybe, much incentive.

Years after my brothers had grown to adulthood, Dad would say, "the biggest mistake I made in my life was not teaching those boys music. It would have been easy once in a while to say, 'Boys, we are going to go in from the fields early today and learn some music,' but I never got around to it."

Despite Dad's regrets, it was Momma who got the ball rolling, musically speaking. Dad led the singing at church, and all of the music there was congregational singing. Momma would sometimes ask Dad if he would like to practice a duet with her so they could "sing a special" at church.

"Nope," would be his inevitable reply.

One night at a prayer meeting service, with maybe fifteen people in attendance, Merlin Utterback, who was leading the service, asked if anybody had anything more to offer after the testimonies had been given and the prayer time was complete.

"Yes, Mr. Utterback," Momma said, "I would like to sing a song."

And so, with Mr. Utterback's eager approval and Dad's obvious consternation, Momma walked to the front of the church, sat down at the piano, struck a chord, and started singing,

"What a friend we have in Jesus, all our sins and griefs to bear; what a privilege to carry everything to God in prayer."

That really did get the ball rolling. At the very next prayer meeting, Tom Knapp, who was leading the service asked first thing, "Mrs. Dodd, do you have a song for us tonight?" and she did. And she did every service after that, every time she was asked. Dad's attitude changed gradually from consternation to grudging acceptance to genuine interest to enthusiastic support, and then he wanted to get in on it.

Duet practice became their favorite pastime. They sang every song they could find which was written for two parts with Dad singing the lead and Momma singing alto on some and Momma singing soprano and Dad singing tenor on others. Now, when Momma was asked if she had a song, she would say with a satisfied smile, "Arthur and I will sing."

At this time, Rhodetta was very proficient at the piano and the three of them started to become recognizable resources in the churches in our area. We would go to a neighboring church during their revival services and either the pastor or the evangelist would spot them and say, "I see that Brother and Sister Dodd are with us tonight. Brother Dodd, would y'all be willing to share a song with us tonight?"

Dad would smile, nod his assent, and immediately lick his thumb as he began turning the pages through that church's hymnal to find the song he wanted to sing. In a few minutes, the preacher would say, "now we are going to hear a song from Brother and Sister Dodd," and Dad would hand a book to Rhodetta opened at the selected song and she would accompany them on the piano as they sang (after Momma gave a testimony, of course).

And boy, could they sing. *"It pays to serve Jesus, it pays every day,"* they would sing. *"Neath the old olive trees, neath the old olive trees, went the Savior alone on His knees,"* and *"There was one who was willing to die in my stead,"* are words which still reverberate through my mind in the clear, pure, two-part harmony which I heard so often.

They didn't just sing, they communicated; Momma through her heart-felt testimonies and Dad through his emotional singing. When a particularly touching part of a song would be reached, Dad's voice would crack and tears would roll down his face. By the time they were finished, there would not be a dry eye in the house. It is easy to understand why evangelists were glad to see them in the audience and would save them for the last thing before the sermon? What better way to prepare a crowd?

When Johnny Cash and June Carter Cash had such a big hit with the song "Daddy Sang Bass, Momma Sang Tenor," I knew what they were singing about because I had been there. Every summer, we would leave our church on two Sundays so we could attend homecomings at Dad's childhood church at Jumping Branch and at Momma's church at Pluto.

A homecoming Sunday featured all day preaching, singing, and "dinner on the ground." I remember one particular year when Dad, Momma, and my sisters were going to sing as a quartet at the homecoming service at Momma's church. All the way there in our old Model A Ford, they practiced. Leora sang soprano, Rhodetta sang alto, and yes, Daddy sang bass and Momma sang tenor and if I had had a little brother, we surely would have joined right in there.

I can still see them that day, with Rhodetta playing the old church pump organ and the other three standing around her as they sang, *"I'll be Somewhere List'ning For My Name,"* in the same little church where Momma had taken Dad's arm one fateful night, many years before.

Momma and Dad both "knew" music. By this, I mean that they could read the notes and sing them, they could both sing either melody or harmony, they could read the music and play it on the keyboard of an organ or piano, and if the key was too high or too low to suit them, they could transpose it into a key which was just right. I grew up taking this for granted, but I have since realized that these two people whose formal education ended with the eighth grade could easily do things musically which some people who had studied music for years could not do. How did this happen?

They had been raised in a time and place where there was an annual event in their churches called a "Singing School." This was a two week event in which a person who was knowledgeable would teach the people of a community the fundamentals of music. A couple of hours a night for two weeks - about twenty hours of instruction - and people would end up reading notes, singing parts, comprehending timing and rhythms, and even learning to play instruments? Sound impossible? Stay with me, I will try to explain how it happened.

First, that which was learned in the Singing School was put into practice at least weekly by those who attended church. Second, the process was repeated annually and the learning was reinforced and built upon. Third, and this one is a key, there was a simplified method to learning music which many people today have only heard about. If it was so simple then, I should be able to explain it now, shouldn't I? Well, I will do just that after another story or two.

From the time I was eleven years old, I was the only child in our home since my two brothers and my two sisters had now gotten married. Before Rhodetta had gotten married, she took me with her one summer to Mrs. Nash, her piano teacher in Alderson, and with a few lessons I learned where the notes were on the scale and a some other bare essentials for beginning to play the piano.

After Rhodetta's marriage, my formal piano training stopped but I continued to "mess around" on the piano and began learning some simple songs. Played mostly "by ear" and in the key of C (all white notes), I could knock out a fast, loud rendition of "Down Yonder" and other tunes of the day with the best of them. To me, the piano just seemed to be a big toy and a diversion from farm work. My introduction into the "real world" came suddenly one night after Rhodetta had gotten married and Dad, Momma, and I were at a revival meeting at the Pence Springs Community Church.

"I see that Brother and Sister Dodd are with us tonight," Evangelist Les Garten announced. "Brother Dodd, would y'all be willing to share a song with us tonight?"

Dad immediately moistened his thumb and began his search through the hymn book during a congregational song while I continued to enjoy myself looking around checking out the pretty girls, totally unaware that disaster was about to strike. When the preacher said, "Now Brother and Sister Dodd will come and minister to us in song," suddenly, without warning, I received a death sentence as Dad thrust an open hymn book into my hands and said, "Here, boy. Play this."

With cold, shaky hands, I got them started in the right key and usually found the ending notes for each verse, but everything in between was a disaster. As we went back to our seats, I was no longer checking out the crowd, looking for girls. I walked back with my head down and scrunched down as low in my seat as possible, wishing I could disappear. I knew that I would never marry anyone in that congregation.

Dad and I had a long talk on the way home that night and we reached a compromise agreement that he would make me a list of songs which I could practice and that I could have veto power over the really hard ones. And then, of course, he forgot about the agreement. From that time on, revival meetings were more of a traumatic nightmare for me than an enjoyable girl-watching opportunity.

It was about this time that Momma and Dad announced that we were going to do something that we should have done a long time ago. We were going to have a Singing School at our church. Their idea was readily accepted by the church and Dad was asked to lead it but he declined and arranged for his friend, Tom Epperly, from the community of Madams Creek, to be the instructor.

I did not know it at the time, but this was during the twilight of the phenomena known as "Singing Schools." Looking back, I consider that one of the great blessings I have received in my life was the opportunity to participate in this form of worship and learning. I did not have to attend many nights until I began to understand how it was that my parents knew so much about music. Music is not a great mystery. It's not that hard! I quickly began to understand more and more of it for myself.

Each year throughout my adolescence, Singing Schools became a regular part of my life, both at our church and also at other churches in the area. Tom Epperly, O. O. Kidd, and the legendary Professor J. A. Lesley became my teachers and heroes.

I quickly discovered that Singing Schools were more than music instruction, much more. Often our church would have more baptisms following a Singing School than after a revival meeting. The music attracted a crowd, the songs pointed to the Savior, and the schools were led by people who let the Holy Spirit lead them to present the Gospel as part of the instruction and give an invitation to receive Christ when it seemed appropriate.

Now, let's talk about the music instruction. How, in the name of

Tom Epperly, O. O. Kidd, or Professor Leslie could a church full of people who know nothing about music learn enough in twenty hours of instruction and practice to lift the roof off the church with beautiful four-part harmony, singing songs they had never heard before?

How? By getting down to basics in the simplest form possible. Back in about 1790, John Connelly of Philadelphia developed a ridiculously simple method of reading music.

His method was published by William Little and William Smith in Albany, New York, around 1800, as *"The Easy Instructor; or a New Method of Teaching Sacred Music."* These men, capitalizing on the fact that there only seven different tones in any scale, gave each its own distinctive shape.

This meant that a person only had to recognize seven shapes to read music that was printed with the shaped notes. How could it be simpler? By contrast, a person had to recognize twenty-six different shapes just to learn the alphabet.

The first night of my first Singing School was a typical first night with Mr. Epperly teaching us seven shapes and identifying them with the notes of the scale, *do, re, mi, fa, sol, la, ti,* and then *do* again.

He described the shapes of the notes as follows: *Do* is a housetop (triangle), *re* is a shoe heel (the letter "u" with a line across the top), *mi* is a baseball field (diamond), *fa* is half a book (right triangle), *sol* is a ball (round), *la* is a book (rectangle), *ti* is an ice cream cone (cone), and that brought us back to *do*.

In later years, when Professor Leslie taught in our area, he would "accidentally" drop his seven large cardboard cutouts in the shape of the notes and have preschool kids help him by picking up the correct shapes. Kids who could not yet read words nor even knew the alphabet were beginning to read music in a matter of minutes.

Once the shapes were learned, the next step was to begin to vocalize them in relation to each other. Mr. Epperly drew the notes onto the lines of a staff which had been painted on a blackboard and had everyone begin singing the scale, first up and then down as he pointed out each note with his baton.

After this became routine, the baton would skip around on the scale. This took a little more effort. Not only did the note have to be identified out of sequence, the correct tone had to be zeroed in on, also. *Do-mi-sol-do* was easy. *Do-la-fa-re* was harder.

Drill, drill, drill; practice, practice, practice. Over and over, night after night, until it became automatic. Not too tough, though, since we only had to learn seven shapes and seven sounds. By the third night this had been largely accomplished.

By listening to people as they sang up and down the scale, Mr. Epperly determined the voice range of everybody. The women with high voices were then seated in the front of the church on the instructor's right and told that they were sopranos. The women with low voices, altos, were seated in the front on the instructors left. The men with high voices, tenors, were seated behind the sopranos and the men with the low voices, basses, were located behind the altos.

At my first Singing School, my voice had not yet changed, and I was placed, much to my horror, in the soprano section. Momma was the leader of the alto section, and poor Dad had developed laryngitis and could only listen. Over the years, as my voice changed, I next joined the tenor section and lastly, to my great satisfaction, the grand and glorious bass section.

Once Mr. Epperly had us properly grouped, he drew some notes on the board and asked the bass group to sing them as he pointed them out with his baton. *"Do do do sol do do do,,, dodododododo do sol, do."* A few times through, a little bit of embarrassed laughter, and soon everyone from the grizzled old men to the bashful teenaged boys were belting it out.

Next the tenors. This was a little harder. *"Mi mi mi sol sol sol sol,,, mimimifasol sol fa, mi."* A few times through and they began to get it. Now the fun began - the basses and tenors were asked to sing at the same time. Different words and different sounds, but strangely they began to blend together in a pleasant pattern. After a few minutes of repetition the two different groups were trying to outdo each other.

Now, the altos. *"Sol sol sol ti do mi do,,, solsolsolsoldo do ti, do."* The women were either quicker on the uptake than the men or they were less easily embarrassed or, maybe it was Momma's leadership because they got it in a hurry and soon three parts of harmony were blending without the benefit of the melody line or an instrument.

We sopranos quickly mastered our part. *"Do do do re mi sol mi,,, dododoremi mi re, do,"* which turned out to be the familiar tune of the first line of "Nothing But the Blood of Jesus." Now all four parts could be blended together, each group singing their own line of music on the board and each naming their own notes, and "lightbulbs of insight" began flashing all over the congregation as we suddenly started to "get it."

Women with low voices who had always hesitated to sing because they could not reach the high notes of a song's melody now realized that they could sing comfortably and beautifully by reading the second line on the staff and sounding the unique notes that were placed there just for them.

Deep voiced men who had before only droned out the tune an octave or two lower than it was written suddenly discovered that singing bass is easier than singing the tune, and you only have to know two notes for this song. It was easy to go to the second line since it was the same as the first and now the group was clamoring to try the chorus.

Before the first week was over a book of new songs was introduced and night after night, first one section and then another went over their line of music until it is mastered and then they were put together, first by singing the notes, and then by singing the words.

Other things were taught including timing, rhythm, chords, and an introduction to the piano. Of course, a person could not be taught proficiency on the piano during this time, but if a person learned that the distance between each note on the piano is a half-step and that a major scale consists of a step, a step, a half step, a step, a step, a step, a half step, they know enough to begin work like my parents did when they were young.

Then when you learned that a major chord is composed of the first, third, and fifth notes of the scale and that a minor chord is simply the same with the third note flatted (lowered a half step), you knew enough to become dangerous. And since you were only working with seven shapes, you could place them anywhere on the piano you chose and transposing to another key was no problem.

Put *do* anywhere you please, count your steps and half steps to identify the scale, and then play the song. Momma liked to play in the keys in which the *do* was on a white key. That meant that regardless of where the music was written, she would play it in the key of her choosing to fit her voice and her fingers.

We learned all sorts of neat stuff which never leaves a person. I know that the spaces on the treble clef are *F, A, C, E,* because that spells face.

The lines on the treble clef are *E, G, B, D, F,* because Every Good Boy Does Fine.

The spaces on the bass clef are *A, C, E, G,* because All Cows Eat Grass, and the lines on the bass clef are *G, B, D, F, A,* because Good Boys Do Fine Always.

Keys with flats, in order of the number of flats in the signature, are *F, B, E, A, D, G,* because Fat Boys Eat Apple Dumplings Greedily.

Just to prove that one does not retain everything forever, even if learned in a Singing School, I have forgotten the snappy saying that correlates to the keys with sharps.

Boy, was that ever a great idea that Momma and Dad had! That first Singing School transformed a community and beyond. People from other communities who had visited our Singing School started planning for similar events in their churches and there was music everywhere.

A few weeks after our first Singing School, Momma and Dad invited neighbors, Elmer and Christie Graham and Pearl Utterback, to our house one Friday night for some fellowship, iced tea, and a piece of Momma's chocolate cake. They had not been there very long until out came the song books and they started to sing, and they didn't stop until after eleven o'clock.

As they were leaving, Elmer and Christy said, "this was so much fun, let's do it again next Friday at our house." And we did, and were joined by a few more of our neighbors. And the next week even more gathered at the Utterbacks, and the next week at someone else's home and on and on for the next ten years or so.

The group grew to a choir of more than thirty people who crowded into a small living room every Friday night for about four hours and sang their hearts out. If the host family had a piano, that was great, and if they did not have a piano, that was great, too. In the absence of a piano, Dad would just look at the key of the song, do a *"sol do mi do sol do,"* and we would start singing. We were so enthusiastic about music that one of the great events of the year was the annual issuing of the latest Stamps-Baxter book of gospel songs.

It wasn't long until we became regular participants at the monthly Summers County Singing Convention. There, amidst the pulsating gospel quartets, the refined soloists, and the "piano-pickin'" instrumentalists, the Griffith Creek Choir took its place. As Singing

Schools were held in other churches, other choirs joined in the Convention; Pence Springs, Rollynsburg, Beech Run, and on and on. Dad even served as President of the Singing Convention for a few years.

Occasionally, we branched out and went to a Singing Convention is another county. I will never forget our first trip to the Greenbrier County Singing Convention. One of the first groups to sing that day was the well-known Midland Trail Quartet, and they opened with their signature song, "Looking For the Stone," which was spectacular. As they got to singing about "looking for the stone that came rolling out of Babylon," they suddenly separated and started roaming throughout the audience looking for the elusive "stone" behind every bench, table, and fat person, never missing a note and filling the church with their harmony.

After a few plaintive verses accompanying their "looking", they joyfully announced that they had "found the stone," and then reunited at the front of the church to jubilantly sing that "Jesus is the stone," after which the crowd erupted and cheered and applauded until they did an encore. I had seen encore calls like this before a few times when the Gilliam Quartet from Beckley had come to our Summers County Convention, so I was not surprised.

What did surprise me, though, was that after the first number by the Griffith Creek Choir, the applause continued as we went to our seats, continued after we sat down, and continued until Dad got up, motioned for us to return to the front of the church and we did an encore. After that was over, we had to do another. A double encore and it was happening to us. I could not believe it.

At the conclusion of that wonderful day, a number of people came to Dad to congratulate him for his choir. One of the members of the Midland Trail Quartet shook Dad's hand and told him that, "the most beautiful voice in the church today belonged to that woman singing alto in the front row of your choir."

That woman was Momma.

11 SUNDAY IS THE LORD'S DAY, SO YOU'D BETTER GET READY ON SATURDAY

"Was a nice day. Had a good Sunday School and Bro. Smith brought a real good message on 'Jesus the Door.' Leora, Les, and children were there. James, Mary and children took dinner with us. Charlotte called and said Jr. was real sick with a headache. Bro. Smith brought another good message, 'Jesus Only.'"
Momma's diary: Sunday, January 12, 1958

"I cleaned up the house, baked a cake, made cheese, dressed a chicken, and prepared things for Sunday dinner."
Momma's diary: Saturday, June 6, 1958

As I have read and reread Momma's diary, two things jump out at me: the importance of Sunday as a day of worship and family togetherness and the importance of Saturday as a day of preparation for Sunday.

Growing up, I only saw Sundays from my own perspective. Sunday was, far and away, the best day of the week. For one thing, we did not work on Sunday except for the necessary chores of milking and caring for the livestock, morning and evening. The morning chores were done before breakfast, so after breakfast I had a free hour or two to read some of the precious books which had accumulated in our house over the years.

Then we would dress in our "Sunday best" and go to Sunday School every Sunday and stay for "preaching" services if it was a "preaching Sunday." Our small church could not afford a full-time pastor, instead, we would call a pastor who served another church or two or three, so we had "preaching" only one or two Sundays a month.

After church we would return home and, within thirty minutes or so, sit down to a feast, nearly always shared with the preacher, some family members, and maybe some neighbors. I would then spend the afternoon with friends or cousins or nieces and nephews, intermittently playing and returning to the kitchen for more dessert.

One of Momma's typical Sunday dinners would include two or three meat dishes. Chicken, either fried, roasted, or boiled with dumplings, was usually one of them and the others would be beef in the form of a roast or Momma's own pan fried, steamed steak, or leg of lamb, or pork, or a wild game meat that was the result of one of our hunting trips.

To complement the meat dishes, there would be gravy, mashed potatoes, macaroni and cheese, and assorted vegetables, always including brown beans. Added to this would be cottage cheese, beet pickles, cucumber pickles, deviled eggs, and during the summer, sliced tomatoes, cole slaw, cantaloupe, and sliced onions.

There were always fresh biscuits and corn bread and, often, rolls and a loaf of home made light bread. To help in the enjoyment of the bread assortment would be home churned butter, honey, sorghum, jams, jellies, and preserves. And then, Momma would serve her desserts. Typically, there would be a cake, some pies, canned fruit, and after we got electricity, ice cream which she had made in the refrigerator and kept smooth by frequent stirring and enriched by generous additions of pure sweet cream until it was perfect.

It probably does not make sense to you that anyone could ever take this kind of event for granted, but I did. This was the Sunday tradition into which I was born, appropriately, on a Sunday. Sunday was a day for little work, some free time, church in the morning and evening, and good times in between. That is what it was from my perspective. What was it from Momma's?

Momma really started preparing for Sunday on Monday. Whether she was a Sunday School teacher or in Dad's adult class, she studied the lesson for the following Sunday as part of her Monday morning Bible reading and prayer time so she could ponder it all week. On Thursday, she walked the mile to the church and gave it a thorough cleaning. And then on Saturday, the real preparations began. Listen to her as she speaks from her diary, now in her sixties, still struggling to recover

from a total nervous breakdown she had experienced just a year before:
*"It snowed 2 in. last night, The sun is shining and snow melting. I
cleaned up the house, churned, and baked pies for tomorrow."*
Saturday, February 8, 1958

Momma began nearly every Saturday entry with, "I cleaned up the
house." Not only was she concerned about having food for Sunday, she
wanted her house to look its best. So she would sweep, dust, and mop
until everything was shining. When I was small and accompanying her
on her weekly cleaning of the church on Thursdays, she would often
remark, "I don't feel right if God's house is not just as clean as my
house," which means that she kept God's house pretty clean, too.

Churning was not necessarily a Saturday job. Churning took place
whenever the cream was ready. If you know someone who was raised
in the country during the 1950's or earlier, they will tell you that they
still miss the taste of "country butter" and they don't know why. Even if
they buy the finest of creamery butter today, the taste is not the same.
The simple reason is that the "country butter" that they are so nostalgic
about was made by churning sour cream and today's butter is made
from sweet cream, and that makes all the difference in the world.

The next time you order a baked potato in a restaurant and you are
asked if you want sour cream and butter, remember that if you only had
some of Momma's hand churned butter, made from sour cream, you
would have the taste of both in one wonderful spread.

Momma churned the old fashioned way most of her life. She used
a five gallon crockery churn with a fitted crockery lid which had a hole
in the center for the handle of the dasher to come up through. The
dasher at the bottom of the handle was made of two crossed wooden
pieces with holes in the four ends to increase the churning action. She
would fill the churn about half full with a rich mixture of cream and
milk which had soured to her personal satisfaction and then sit and
churn until the heaviness on the dasher told her that the butter had
formed.

She would then remove the clumps of butter from the churn,
"work" it with her hands to remove any liquid, salt it, roll just the right
amount into a ball and throw it with her right hand sharply into a
wooden butter printer held in her left hand. Then she would turn the
printer upside down on a saucer, and by pushing down on the false

bottom of the printer, create a beautiful pound of butter, perfectly molded and with the imprint of a pineapple on top.

Like magic, she created the perfect complement for hot bread, baked potatoes, or sweet corn. Oops, don't forget the churn, it is still half full of buttermilk, the irreplaceable ingredient in all of Momma's bakery items and a refreshing drink on a hot summer day.

As for baking the pies, this was a weekly ritual. Baking pies, and preparing other food items for Sunday occupied most of her time after she had "cleaned up the house" every Saturday. Let me take you through some more excerpts from her diary:

"It has been a pretty day. I baked three pies, deviled some eggs, and made cheese for Sunday." March 7, 1958

The "cheese" Momma mentions making is cottage cheese, made from clabbered milk by separating the curds from the whey and squeezing the curds in a cloth to get them dry and crumbly and then seasoning them just right with a bit of pepper.

"Another nice day. I prepared some things for Easter dinner. Haven' t felt very well this afternoon." April 4, 1958

"Some things for Easter" would consist of Momma's normal preparation for Sunday plus an emphasis on eggs. Easter was the one day when we did not skimp on egg consumption. Regardless of how much they could be sold for, Easter was a day for eating eggs. One challenge which I was never able to achieve although I tried mightily every Easter, was to match what Dad said that his brother Reggie had accomplished when they were young; Reggie had eaten a dozen of eggs for breakfast one Easter morning. The best that I could ever do was to eat a dozen during the entire day.

So preparing for Easter meant that a large supply of eggs must be on hand. On the Saturday before Easter, a dozen or two hardboiled eggs would already be in a gallon jar in the refrigerator covered with pickled beets, soaking up the colorful, spicy pickle juice, creating the most beautiful, tasty eggs in the universe. Momma would boil another dozen or two and make deviled eggs on Saturday, and plenty more had to be reserved for the one big egg breakfast of the year.

119

"It rained most all afternoon. . . . baked three cherry pies and light bread. Killed a chicken. Got a nice Mother's day card from Paul."   May 9, 1958

". . . baked light bread, picked some peas and beans for Sunday dinner. Have felt better today."   June 20, 1958

". . . dressed two young roosters . . ." August 23, 1958

When Momma said that she "dressed two young roosters," this means that she sprinkled some grains of corn in the chicken yard and while the chickens were eating, she selected and deftly grabbed a young fryer sized rooster. She then held him by the feet in her left hand, positioned his head on a chopping block, and wielding a man-sized double-bitted axe with her right hand, chopped off his head with one swift blow. Then, while that one was flopping around "like a chicken with its head cut off," she selected and caught another and did the same thing again.

Next, she scalded them in boiling water to loosen the feathers and she "picked" them, or removed the feathers. She then built a small paper fire and rotated each of them over the fire to "singe" or burn off the hairs. Now she was ready to remove the insides, saving the livers and gizzards, and cut the chickens into the sized pieces she wanted for frying.

"I have been real busy today. Baked eight apple pies for our Sunday School picnic tomorrow and a banana cake for home use. Canned some peaches and two jars vegetable soup. Gathered and strung a peck of beans for tomorrow. I am tired tonight."
August 30, 1958

". . . dressed a fryer, scrubbed the smoke house and arranged things so it is clean. I baked a cake and two apple pies this afternoon. Peeled some apples to dry."   September 20, 1958

Momma dried apples by placing apple slices on a framed window screen and anchoring the screen on the warming shelf of her wood-burning cook stove with flat irons. In this way, the screen extended out over the stove eighteen or so inches above the cooking surface. When the apple slices were completely dried, they were put into empty round oatmeal boxes and stored in the pantry until needed for pies or other apple desserts during the winter. She used the same procedure to dry green beans and sweet corn.

> ". . . made a cake and four pies (2 apple and 2 pumpkin) before noon. Worked on the yard some and picked a bucket of beans. It turned cold and I thought it might frost. I am ready for bed."
>
> September 27, 1958

> ". . . baked a cake and three pies. Tried to get things ready for Sunday. Churned and raked leaves in the afternoon."
>
> October 11, 1958

I think you get the idea. By working all day Saturday preparing her house and the bulk of her food for Sunday, all Momma had to do on Sunday was to get her stove hot, and while she was preparing breakfast, start frying the chicken, put the roast in the oven, cook the beans and other vegetables, peel the potatoes, stir the ice cream one more time and add cream, and then after breakfast make the fresh biscuits and corn bread which could be wrapped and left in the still warm oven after baking and be just right for dinner.

By doing things this way, "all" she had to do when we got home from church was to rebuild the fire, warm up all the precooked foods, boil and mash the potatoes, make the gravy, and serve the meal. She could usually rely on us to set the table.

On the Sundays when we would observe the Lord's Supper at church, she would also bake the unleavened bread. She would prepare a mixture of ingredients similar to her biscuit dough, only without baking powder, roll it out thin, place it in a pan, score it with the tines of a fork, and bake it. The result was a simple, crisp flat bread which Momma would break into small squares along the lines of tiny holes she had made with the fork tines. She would wrap this in a cloth napkin and take it along with a jar of her best homemade grape juice for the Communion service.

Why did she do all this? There were probably a number of

reasons. She had been raised in a very large family and in a home which usually had company for Sunday dinner, so this was what she had been taught by her mother. By being a member of a large family, unannounced visits by two or three carloads of relatives from her side of the family or from Dad's side was not unusual, and sometimes they both got there the same day.

Her standard response to a situation of a large group of unexpected company was, "I don't know if we will have enough to eat but I'll just trust the Lord to multiply what we have," and it seemed like he always did. But Momma always started out with a lot more food than Jesus did on the day he fed the multitude with two loaves and five fish (or was it five loaves and two fish?). And she had a cellar full of canned meats, vegetables, and fruits which could be quickly added to the menu, if needed. But after the day was successfully over, she would always give all the credit to God. "I was worried about it for awhile," she would say, "but I knew that the Lord would multiply it and he did!" And she would rejoice.

I remember getting into big trouble at the Sunday dinner table once when I was small. As the youngest person at the table, it was logical that I was the last person to whom the food was passed. When the fried chicken was passed to me, I expressed my unhappiness that there was not any breast left. I was quietly urged to select a drumstick or thigh but, for some reason, I had my heart set on white meat that day so I started to throw a tantrum. Bad strategy! Dad almost jerked my arm out of its socket as we abruptly began our trip out to the woodshed.

Before he walloped me, he said, "Boy, didn't you see that the whole chicken breast was on Brother Ward's plate? Do you know how bad you made him feel? Did you see the look on his face when you started squallin'? Let me tell you something, boy, I didn't know that a chicken had anything but a neck 'til I was eighteen years old." After that experience, the drumstick, thigh, and even the neck looked a whole lot better to me.

One thing for sure was that the chicken breast was not on Momma's plate. She always opted for one of the "lesser" pieces. On a day when the dinner crowd was small, she would choose a wing. When the crowd was larger she would say, "Save me the neck."

Her granddaughter, Mary Carol, was intrigued by this strange choice of chicken parts which was reinforced by Dad telling her once,

"Save the neck for your Grandma, that's her favorite piece." When Mary Carol got older she just had to ask her Grandma why the neck was her favorite piece of chicken. "Why, that's not my favorite piece of chicken, Honey," Momma told her. "I don't even like the neck, I just take it so other people can have the better pieces."

Now, in Mary Carol's family, when someone sees the need to do some sacrificial or unselfish act, the operative phrase is "just save me the neck."

"We has three inches of snow by church time and roads were slippery. We went to Sunday School and preaching. Bro. Smith brought a good message. He took dinner with us. James's could not get up the hill so they came back and ate with us, then walked home. Rhodetta, Ralph and children came."
Sunday, December 14, 1958

Now, I know that you are asking, "what happened if there was no company to help eat all that food?" The simple answer is that we sure ate good for the rest of that week. Nothing was ever wasted and an abundance of food to warm over during the following week made Momma's cooking job easier and gave her more time to hoe the garden, pick cherries, make apple butter, or help put hay in the barn, and those pies and cakes just seemed to get better and better as the week went along.

I still love leftovers. They are like a gift. They have already been paid for, so to speak, so it is like eating for nothing. I am not sure if leftovers have less calories, but they should so they could be eaten totally guilt-free. I like brown beans warmed over until they get mushy, I love leftover mashed potatoes fried into crisp, brown potato cakes, I like day-old corn bread crumbled up in a glass of milk, and I enjoy a piece of cake even if there is a bit of a crust forming on the once creamy frosting.

But on those weekdays after there was a lot of company for Sunday dinner and the feast was consumed, we ate a lot more of whatever was in season at the time, like turnips, parsnips, cabbage, etc., in other words, stuff that did not qualify in my book as feast material.

That did not matter, though. I would gladly live out my week days on such food if I could only experience again the wonder of family and

123

friends together around Momma's big dining room table on Sunday. This is the way she described one of those great days:

"Arthur and I went to Sunday School. Paul went after Rosie but they didn't get to church. They were keeping house when we got home. James, Mary, and children stopped. Jr., Charlotte, Rhodetta, Ralph, and children all came. Leora, Les, and children got back from Stanaford. We had a good dinner (I guess).

Sunday, November 2, 1958

Yes, Momma, I guess we did!

12   "DOCTOR, I DON'T KNOW WHY I AM HERE,
I AM A CHRISTIAN!"

*"It has been a nice day. The men worked in the hay, finishing three patches. James, Claude, Paul, and Arthur worked hard and late to get it done. I did my work and cooked for them. **This time last year I was very sick and couldn't take very much noise.** I am thankful to be lots better."*

Momma's diary: June 5, 1958

Momma had great respect for doctors, and she was actually a pretty good doctor in her own right.   There were few maladies that struck her children that could not be treated with her favorite remedies of buttermilk and aspirin to take down a fever, vaporub to break up a chest cold, milk of magnesia and enemas to, well, you know, and when a miracle drug was needed, castor oil.

Using these medicines and procedures, she nursed us through whooping cough, measles, chicken pox, croup, flu, and mumps.   Our skinned knees and stubbed toes were painted liberally (and set on fire) with iodine or merthiolate, and the discomfort of bee stings or poison ivy was relieved (somewhat) by being covered with a paste of baking soda and water.

But, in addition to being proficient in her ability to treat common ailments, somewhere along the line, probably as a product of the times, Momma had gotten the idea that the human body is in need of help.   By this I mean that she believed in "cleansing" the body, inside and out. She believed that vitamins and tonics and "physics" were highly beneficial.   As a matter of fact, she had a great respect for medicine, so much so, that she did not like to see it wasted.

Momma had her own regimen from the time of my first recollections. As soon as the kitchen stove got hot enough to warm the teakettle in the morning, she would drink a cup of warm water "to get her system going." She would have a vitamin or the current "tonic" sometime during the day and then often take an aspirin before going to bed.

Sometimes Momma's belief that the body needed a little help got her into trouble and sometimes it was just funny. When I was very small, I remember going with her and Dad to Dr. Argabright's office in Alderson and hearing the good doctor give her a stern lecture and then hearing Dad add to it on the way home.

The reason Momma had to go to the doctor was that she had broken out in large, itchy welts all over her body, for no apparent reason. Dr. Argabright quickly diagnosed the problem as a reaction to some substance and questioned her about any change in the food she had eaten or anything else she might have put into her system.

"I don't know what it might be," she said, "The only thing that I have been taking is a vitamin pill each day."

"What kind of vitamins are they?" the doctor asked.

"I don't know, exactly," she said, "they were some that my brother left at our house when he visited us last week."

And that was when the doctor started yelling. Momma had seen some pills, assumed that since they were medicine they would help and certainly not hurt a body, so she started taking Uncle Rheo's pills and paid an uncomfortable and embarrassing price.

One Sunday after church when James, Mary, and kids had stopped for dinner, as Mary was helping Momma get the food hot and on the table, she made the mistake of telling Momma that her stomach was a bit upset. "Mary, what you need is some Sal Hepatica," Momma said, "I'll fix you some."

"I can't stand Sal Hepatica," Mary responded, "please don't fix me any for I won't take it."

Undeterred, Momma measured out the proper amount, put it into a glass of water, stirred it, watched it fizz, and then said, "here, Mary, take this. It will make you feel better."

"I hate that stuff," Mary stated emphatically, "and I am not going to take it!"

Momma was momentarily dumbfounded by Mary's adamant response but she quickly recovered. "Well, I don't want to see it go to waste," she said as she turned up the glass and drank it herself.

And then, once upon a time, there was a miracle tonic named Hadacol.

This was Colonel Tom Parker's most successful promotion until he signed on with Elvis Presley and he never promoted Elvis any better than he did Hadacol, although Elvis did have a longer run.

The promotion of Hadacol exceeded anything we had ever seen. It was everywhere, on the radio, in magazines, in the paper, and most of all, in the general conversation. Hadacol jokes were rampant (they had-a-col it something). We heard tales of holes in people's teeth miraculously filling themselves, bald men growing thick, beautiful hair, and even that one man had to carry a hatchet with him at all times to chop off the sprouts that kept growing from his wooden leg.

Momma, for some reason, was reluctant to try Hadacol. After months of hearing about nothing else, though, she finally decided that she just didn't have the energy that she needed and maybe, just maybe, a "run" of Hadacol might help.

Boy, did it! After her first big dose she grabbed a hoe, went into her garden and killed weeds with a fury. Suddenly, nothing was too great a task for her to take on. Gardening, cleaning, cooking, helping with the farm work all were now possible, and all in the same day.

After a few days of this great flurry of activity and Dad assumed that any placebo effect had worn off, he got curious. "Let me see that stuff," he said. "What's it got in it?"

When he read the label, he said, "Law have mercy, child, this stuff is forty percent alcohol. Your tonic is the same as eighty proof whiskey. No wonder you're gettin' a kick out of it."

Of course, that was all it took to end the use of Hadacol at our house. Remember, thou shalt not smoke or chew, and drinking is out of the question, so miracle drug or not, the eighty proof Hadacol had to go.

One of the defining moments of Momma's life was her surviving a terrible bout with Typhoid Fever, early in her marriage. She hovered near death for days with a dangerously high temperature. This episode, in her mind, was a reason for many things. She lost all of her hair and after it grew back, her hair never had any natural oil. During the winters, she shampooed very infrequently and her hair was always uniformly soft and dry. She said that her equilibrium was affected. She was never as steady on her feet as before and, as a result, prone to falling.

She also believed that she was a much more nervous person than before. She believed that this was a factor in the "nervous breakdown" she suffered while she and Dad were taking care of her terminally ill father in our home, before I was born.

Her biggest concern, though, was that it had affected her intellect and that she was not as mentally sharp as she had been before the illness. She told me that when she was a girl, she was always the first one in her class to finish her school work and that she always made the best grades, but after having Typhoid Fever, she just was not as smart as she was before. She was especially frustrated by math, which had been her favorite subject in school. I remember the difficulty she had with getting the timing right on new music. She could explain the difference between the eighth, quarter, and half notes, but had a difficult time putting the knowledge into practice.

My perception is that, despite the likelihood of some diminishing of Momma's intellect due to the high temperature she endured, she was still one of the most intelligent people I have ever known. However, in her own mind, because she was comparing her mental capacity after the illness to her mental capacity before the illness, she believed that she was lacking in intelligence, and often put herself down.

She was too smart for any of us to ever put anything over on her. I can't imagine how tough she would have been at full steam. She sure would have been something!

During my lifetime I have taken, and even taught, courses which are designed to sharpen the mind and improve memory. Sometimes when I would be presented with a technique, I would recognize it as one that Momma had used, without the benefit of the current "wonder course." For example, I know that she used the "association method" to help her remember names.

Teachers of the association method tell you to, when confronted with a new word or name, associate the new word or name with something familiar. A simple illustration of this would be if you are introduced to someone named Smith, picture that person in a blacksmith shop, doing the work of a smithy. Other easy names to remember by obvious association would be Farmer, Miner, Rivers, etc. Less obvious names require more creativity in picturing the person in a memorable way which will forever remind you of the name.

I once had an unexpected visitor stop in the office where I was working in Princeton who was a U. S. Department of Agriculture associate from another state who had seen our office sign and decided to stop in and get acquainted. His last name was Studer. Five minutes into our conversation one of my co-workers came in and I tried to introduce them but I could not recall the name, "Studer," so I had to ask him again for his name.

A few minutes more and another co-worker arrived with the same result. Then the boss came in and I began to stammer, blush, and apologize because, once again, I had forgotten his name. How do I remember it now, forty years later? Because after my fourth failure to recall his name, I finally used association, I pictured him getting into a Studebaker car eating a strudel!

The time that I caught Momma using association was when some of her family who were visiting us had brought one of their friends, a Mrs. Underwood, with them to our house. After a most pleasant afternoon of talking and refreshments and the visitors were leaving, Momma bade them farewell with the usual, "Ya'll come back when you can," and then fatally added, "You come back, too, Mrs. Underwear."

As I mentioned before, Momma held medical doctors in high regard, almost on a plane with preachers, missionaries, and Rescue Mission directors. Doctors were among Momma's heroes. Doctors liked Momma, too, especially Dr. Argabright. Despite his consternation at her self-medication on Uncle Rheo's pills, he always asked Momma to help him with the home delivery of any babies in our neighborhood. He told her after each delivery that she was better help than any nurse he had ever worked with.

Psychiatrists, though, were apparently not on the same level with medical doctors in Momma's mind. I do not think that she was particularly negative about them, but she probably did not give them much thought and certainly never entertained the idea that she might someday need the services of one.

She knew about the psychiatric treatment of her brother Claude, who seemed to be as paranoid after treatment as before. She had heard many disparaging references to psychiatry by well-meaning but ignorant preachers and probably had adopted some of their prejudice.

In 1957, during my freshman year in college, Momma developed a serious problem.

I was informed by Dad that Momma had suffered a "nervous breakdown" and that I should not be surprised when I came home, for things were bad. I came home the very next Friday evening to spend the weekend, confident that Momma's baby boy would be of great help and comfort to her and maybe I would be able to cheer her up and get her back to normal.

Did I get a shock. When I arrived, she did not even want me to come into her room. She did not want Dad around, either, nor anyone else. My sisters had tried to help Dad care for her with little success. I opened the door to her room and saw her lying in bed with a terrified look on her face, ready to jump out of her skin. She was highly agitated, alternately crying and hysterically praying.

When she said in her diary that she "could not take very much noise," she was guilty of a gross understatement. She could not stand to hear even the slightest sound so Dad had stopped all the clocks in the house so she would not be agitated by the ticking. Any conversation had to be held outside the house where she could not hear. Care had to be taken in preparing food and eating even though the kitchen was located in the back of the house, far from her bedroom. Any rattle of a pot or pan or clinking of dishes and silverware would send her into a hysterical state.

I was sitting quietly in the living room which adjoined her bedroom Saturday morning when she called to me. "Paul, you have to do something with that rooster. I can't stand to hear him," she cried. "I don't care if you have to shoot him, just do something with him so I don't have to hear him."

Catching a healthy rooster is not an easy task, but I somehow worked him into a fence corner and grabbed him with his wings flapping, his beak squawking, and his spurs flashing and with a minimum loss of blood (mine) I relocated the rooster into one of the stalls of the barn, far out of Momma's earshot.

Sunday morning, Momma seemed a bit calmer so I went out with Dad to help with the chores. When we came back into the house, there was Momma in the kitchen and I momentarily thought that she had snapped out of it. It was quickly evident, though, that she had not snapped out of it at all; she had just snapped. She had a strange look in her eyes and she was talking in a sing-song voice about fixing a "nice little breakfast" and she had poured kerosene all over the stove and was looking for the matches. Dad hid the matches, sat down in a kitchen chair, and cried like a baby.

Early the following week, Dad and Leora told Momma that they were taking her to Beckley to see a doctor. She did not protest too much, although the thought of the hour and a half trip heightened her anxiety even more. Dad was dreading Momma's reaction when she realized that rather than one of her esteemed medical doctors, she was going to see the unthinkable - a psychiatrist. "What'll we do," he wondered, "if she bucks on us when we get there and won't see the doctor?"

Momma's recognition of the type of doctor she was going to see came when she saw the door of the office: Dr. Wilkinson, *Psychiatrist.*

"Is this where we are going?" she asked.

"Yep," Dad told her, "this is the place."

"Then, let's go," she said, as she headed into the office.

When Dr. Wilkinson came into the room where Momma was to be treated, he introduced himself and asked, "Mrs. Dodd, why have you come to see me?"

Momma replied, "Doctor, I don't know why I am here. I should not be here! I am a Christian!"

The Doctor responded, "What do you mean when you say you are a Christian, Mrs. Dodd? Do you mean that you have been saved?"

"Yes," Momma said, and the wise doctor then said, "Tell me about it."

Momma became calm and told the doctor that she had accepted Christ as her Savior when she was a young girl. She told him that she had always prayed and believed that God would never fail to meet her needs. She recounted that when she was in school as a young teenager, after she had finished her work she would lay her head on her desk and people would think that she was resting, but instead, she would be praying.

She said that her greatest desire from that time until now had been to live a life that was pleasing to God. She told him about all of the struggles that she had gone through in her life and that God had always been sufficient. But, now, she told him, she could not understand why this situation had befallen her and her prayers were going unanswered.

"Mrs. Dodd," the doctor asked, "when your body gets sick, even though you pray for God to heal you, do you go to doctors for help?"

"Yes, I do," Momma replied.

"Then I want you to think of me just like you think of the other doctors you trust to help you," he explained. "When your body is sick, you need them to help you. Now your mind is sick and you need me in the very same way and, if you will let me, I can help you."

It was a slow, torturous process. Every two steps of progress was accompanied by at least one step back. Trip after trip had to be made to Beckley, with Momma nearly hysterical during the ride to the doctor and relaxed and at peace on the ride home. But she made it.

Although she was never again as emotionally strong as she had once been, she came a long way back, as evidenced by her activities as chronicled in her diary which she began a year after her "breakdown" and in which she documents her still-ongoing trips to Dr. Wilkinson for her "treatments."

"Arthur took me to Beckley Wednesday afternoon for a treatment. I stayed with Lura until Saturday afternoon. Took another treatment on Thursday and one on Saturday. Doctor could not see me on Friday as he was out of town."

Momma's diary: February 25, 1959

Although Momma was never as emotionally strong as she once had been, she learned to pace herself and to know her limits. And just as she learned about herself, we learned a few things about her that we should have already known. One day, in a therapy session, the doctor asked, "Mrs. Dodd, what is the worst thing you can imagine?"

Her reply told volumes. This woman who had always worked to her limit and beyond, who had always welcomed family, friends, and even dirty strangers with infested dogs into her home, who had always prepared in anticipation of unexpected guests, replied, "the worst thing that I can imagine is to be coming home from church and when we drive across the bridge and get in sight of our house I see three or four carloads of people waiting for Sunday dinner."

Wow! My favorite scenario turned out to be Momma's worst nightmare.

As with all of the other "good news" that Momma had, she openly shared her experiences with psychiatry with others and assured anyone who was dealing with mental or emotional problems that God had provided psychiatrists and their treatments as an answer to prayer just as certainly as he had provided medical doctors and medicines to provide healing for the body.

I related Momma's experience to an evangelist who had just lambasted psychiatrists in his sermon, roughly equating them with witchcraft and demons. I didn't get through to him, though. He quickly got rid of me by saying, "Praise the Lord! She found a Christian psychiatrist. There are not many of them. Do you know how lucky she was? Hallelujah!" and he was done with the subject and with me.

His reaction and closed-mindedness really angered me. I just finally had to accept that the Apostle Paul was right: light and darkness do not have much fellowship. I am still troubled that a pompous preacher would lightly pass off the reality of God's blessings to one of his servants merely because it did not fit his narrow point of view.

I do not know what the beliefs of Momma's doctor were. He may have been a Christian, and he probably was. But he may have been a Buddhist for all I know, for I have known people who have been helped by psychiatrists of that religion. What I do know is that he was a skilled and sensitive healer who knew the culture of the person he was treating, accurately analyzed her, met her on familiar ground, and was God's instrument in providing healing to Momma in answer to her prayers.

Momma's last medical problem was one which would not respond to treatment or go away. By the time it was finally diagnosed, Parkinson's Disease had advanced to the point of no return and Momma's condition gradually worsened until she was "called home" on that day after Thanksgiving in 1976.

Momma was not well six years earlier when James passed away but we did not know the cause or extent of her infirmities. Her condition continued to deteriorate after his death and this was attributed by doctors and family members to her grieving over the loss of her son.

It was nearly a year after James' death when I asked her directly if she thought that the reason for her poor health was her grief, as everyone supposed.

"No, dear," she said, "something is wrong in my brain and I know just when it started. I was on my knees in church, leading in prayer, when something in my head snapped. I don't know if it was a little stroke, or a broken blood vessel, or what, but something happened then and I haven't been the same since."

By the time the doctors figured out what was wrong, her hands were permanently half closed, her walk was a shuffle, and her body was becoming stooped and rigid.

The doctors told Dad what we could expect. He was told that there would be a drastic change in her personality and not to be surprised if Momma became very negative and unpleasant as her condition advanced. I talked to other people who had experienced this and similar diseases with their loved ones and found that the doctor's prognosis usually came true.

One of my friends told me of his father who went through a complete personality change. His father was a minister and social activist. He had been one of the early supporters of the civil rights movement and had marched with Dr. King. My friend had never heard his father utter a vulgar word nor use a racist phrase. But then, as his mental condition worsened, his attitude and his vocabulary changed drastically. Now, for the first time in his life, my friend heard his father rant and rave, swearing and expressing contempt for people for whom he had once risked his life, referring to them in the most disparaging of terms.

My friend found peace with this situation only after he was made to realize that his father had regressed to his early childhood, a time when he was in the very biased environment of his parents and grandparents. He understood that his father was speaking out of the darkness in which he was reared instead of out of the enlightenment of the changed adult life which he had chosen.

But, despite our fears, this never happened with Momma. She kept her sweet, unselfish personality as long as she was conscious, and beyond. As long as she could speak, every care giver was complimented and thanked by Momma. Even as she regressed to a much earlier time of life in her consciousness, she never regressed to a time of meanness or selfishness. It was as if that time never existed within her.

After Momma went into a coma in August, we assumed that she would not be heard from again, but she had one surprise left. In November, just days before her death, Dad and Leora were visiting her still, tiny, rigid form in the nursing home, with Momma showing no signs of awareness at all when, suddenly she started to sing, and she sang clearly, without missing a word of this old song:

> *"There's not a friend like the lowly Jesus,*
> *No, not one! No, not one!*
> *None else could heal all our soul's diseases,*
> *No, not one! No not one!*
> *Jesus knows all about our struggles,*
> *He will guide till the day is done;*
> *There's not a friend like the lowly Jesus,*
> *No, not one! No, not one!"*

"Momma! You can still sing, can't you?" Leora exulted as Dad stood sobbing. "That was beautiful."

No response, at least not visibly. She just lay there, staring blankly into space, her mouth gaped wide. But somehow Momma had used some little corner of her brain that was still functioning and with it she did a marvelous thing. She not only sang praises to her Savior, she also gave a powerful testimony of her faith and provided an unforgettable farewell message to her beloved ones.

13 MESSAGES FROM MOMMA,
AS SHE LEFT THEM IN HER BIBLES

"We are all living because of the Grace of God."
Written by Momma in an old Bible

Since Momma felt led to write things down, she must have intended for someone to read them. I want to devote the last chapter of this book to some of the things which I found written in the inside covers of her Bibles, on lined tablet sheets folded and left in the old Bibles, and on assorted other scraps of paper. Some of these writings are quotes from scripture, some are words from songs, some are copies of thoughts from sources which are unknown to me, and some are her original thoughts. The capitalization and underlining which I show are hers. In a few cases, she identifies herself by signing her name, initials (B. D.), or title (Mother), to her writings.

Put together, these writings give a composite picture of Momma's deep faith, her love for God, and her devotion to others. Listen as she shares a testimony of her innermost thoughts with you which I have grouped under various topics.

The proper order of things for a Child of God:
"Love not the world or the things that are in the world: If any man love the things of the world, the love of the Father is not in him."

"We should not neglect Spiritual things for Material things."

"We must first be partakers of Christ, then labor for Him."

"May God's precious will be done in our lives, to the glorifying of His precious Name."

"May we be able to say, 'it is not I that liveth, but Christ that liveth within me.'"

"Life should be so very serious for us all; but we take it so lightly."

"Just one life, it will soon be past: only what's done for Christ will last."

Salvation:
"By grace are ye saved through faith and that not of yourself, it is the Gift of God."

"The wages of sin is death, but the Gift of God is eternal life through Jesus Christ our Lord."

"The greatest need of every precious soul is, to prepare to meet thy God."

"Father, we thank you for saving grace and keeping power."

God's grace:
"We are all living because of the Grace of God."

"Whosoever means that all who will may accept Christ and be saved."

"Eternal Life through Jesus Christ is the greatest gift that any one can receive."

"It is so wonderful to know that God provided a means to save poor sinners from eternal destruction through Jesus Christ. All who will come to God through Christ shall be saved. That is the only way. We should weep and pray over our lost loved ones now and not wait

137

until they die and then weep and wish that we had tried to win them to Christ."

God's faithfulness:

"The Lord forsaketh not His saints; they are preserved forever. Psa. 37:28

"Saints enter into rest when they die and will be rewarded later."

"God has provided salvation for every soul that will have a repenting heart toward God and Faith in the Lord Jesus Christ."

"We are kept in the will of God, by the power of God, for the Glory of God."

God's promises:

"Precious promises of God unto His children:
Ye that love the Lord, hate evil; He preserveth the souls of His saints; He delivereth them out of the hand of the wicked. Psa. 97:10

The angel of the Lord encampeth around about them that fear Him, and delivereth them. Psa. 34:7

I have set the Lord always before me; because He is at my right hand and shall never be moved. Psa. 16:8

The eye of the Lord is upon the righteous, and His ears are open unto their cry. Psa. 34:15

The whole earth is full of the Glory of God. Isa. 6:3

As the mountains are round about Jerusalem, so the Lord is around about his people, henceforth and forever more.

He shall give His angels charge over thee, to keep thee in all thy ways.

The steps of a good man are ordered by the Lord.

Oh that men would praise the Lord for His goodness, and for his wonderful works to the children of men.

The Lord shall preserve thee from all evil; He will preserve thy soul. Psa. 121:7"

God's deliverance:
"Was able to walk today, May 3, 1954, after being crippled 15 weeks. Am so very thankful to my blessed Lord for healing my body and for all his blessings. May I be faithful and do my best for Him in return. Bless the Lord oh my soul and all that is within me, bless His Holy Name."   *"B. D."*

God's wrath:
"God always warns before He strikes. Surely He is warning us in this day. But people do not believe God or heed his warning. So, He is going to have to pour out His wrath upon us."

Personal responsibility:
"The most important question that ever entered into my mind is my personal responsibility to God. May Thy Holy Spirit abide in our hearts."

"We should live an obedient, God fearing life, loving God with all our soul, strength, and power."

"Lord stir our hearts to do our very best for Thee."

*"Lord, lay some soul upon my heart,
    and love that soul through me;
And may I bravely do my part
    To win that soul for Thee."*

*"Lord, send me anywhere; only go with me.
    Lay any burden upon me; only sustain me.
    Sever any tie save that which binds my heart to Thee."*

"Dear Lord, forgive us for our unconcern for those that are lost about us and all over the world."

Things to avoid:
"There are six things doth the Lord hate. Yea, seven are an abomination unto Him:

>*(1) a proud look*
>*(2) a lying tongue*
>*(3) hands that shed innocent blood*
>*(4) a heart that deviseth wicked imaginations*
>*(5) feet that be swift in running to mischief*
>*(6) a false witness that speaketh lies*
>*(7) he that soweth discord among the brethern"*

The future:
God holds the future in His hands.

Christ's return:
"If Jesus should come at this moment to catch up with Him in the air, all those who love His appearing, forever to be with Him there: How would He find you, I wonder - watching, waiting, faithful, true?"

"Dearly beloved, consider - how would it be with you? 'If my people, which are called by my name, shall humble themselves, and pray, and seek my face, and turn from their wicked ways: then will I hear from heaven, and will forgive their sin, and will heal their land.'"

Starting the New Year right:
"Jan. 1st, 1954 - We are thankful we have lived to see a New Year come in. We had singing and a watch service in our home last evening which was attended by about 20. My refreshments were Kool-Aid and coffee, fruit cake and cookies, candy and apples. All seemed to enjoy the evening. Arthur read scripture - all repeated favorite scripture verses and closed with prayers as 1953 was going out and 1954 being ushered in. I trust we will all seek to do God's will and be ready if God should call us in 1954."

"Bertha Dodd"

Honoring Christ at Christmas:

"Dec. 25th 1955 - We got up at 6 o'clock, had our prayer as usual and opened our gifts which were very nice. All the children were here for dinner and Arthur Jr., took pictures of us all. We had a wonderful day. Our grandchildren - 11 in all - sure had a time together. Before leaving for their homes, Dad prayed a very sweet, impressive prayer. We were all touched and drawn closer to each other and to God.

We pray God will let us all live to be together next Christmas, but should He call any of us, my prayer is that we will be ready to meet our Blessed Savior whose birth we have celebrated once more. May we be an undivided Family around the Blessed Throne of God, where all is Love, Peace, and Happiness."

"Mother"

Love:

"Love is the greatest spiritual gift."

"The Greatest Thing in all the world is the Love of God. May our hearts be motivated by Love from God."

"Love means sacrifice."

"There is something so different in a gift which is born of Love! God gave to man the richest treasure of heaven. He gave because He Loved. Shall we not at least give Him back our lives?"

Faith:

"There is only one step to God. That step is Faith."

"When we exercise what faith God has given us, He will honor it and give us more faith."

Perfection:

We can be perfect only in Jesus Christ. We should be in love with Jesus; who loved us enough to be willing to die for us, to redeem us back to God.

I close this book with a message from Momma, not only to me, but also to you. If you, like me, consider this book to be a sermon from Momma, you realize that it is imperative that she extends an invitation for us to share her faith in God through Christ. Her "precious loved ones," undoubtedly refers to her family but that word "neighbor" is a big one.

Remember that Momma had no enemies and she considered everyone her neighbor. So, take my word for it, Momma is talking to you just as surely as she is talking to me. I also believe that she is joined by countless millions of other Mommas who are with her on the other side, as she extends this message to us, which she wrote on January 1, 1963:

All my Faith and Trust is in Jesus my Savior, who has redeemed my soul by His precious blood on Calvary. I am hid in Him and ready to meet my Blessed Lord at any moment, Praise his Holy Name forever and forever.

I will be watching for each of my precious loved ones and neighbors, should I go first.

Please be faithful - Love and prayers to all.

Bertha Dodd

Amen!

Momma at age 20.

Dad and Momma's wedding picture.

Arthur, Jr., with his "ferocious" dog Trixie.

Author, age 5, with brother James, age 18.

Leora (left) and Rhodetta as teenagers.

The Dodd farm.